Poetry Ireland Review 130

Editor
COLETTE BRYCE

© Poetry Ireland Ltd 2020

Poetry Ireland CLG/Éigse Éireann CTR gratefully acknowledges the assistance of
The Arts Council/An Chomhairle Ealaíon and The Arts Council of Northern Ireland.

Poetry Ireland invites individuals and commercial organisations to become
Patrons of Poetry Ireland. For more details, please contact:
Anne Hendrick, Development Manager,
Poetry Ireland, 11 Parnell Square East,
Dublin 1, Ireland
or telephone +353 1 6789815; e-mail development@poetryireland.ie

FOUNDING PARTNERS
Adrian Brinkerhoff Poetry Fund of the Sidney E Frank Foundation
University College Cork

POETRY PATRONS: LYRIC
Joseph Hassett, Thomas Dillon Redshaw, Ronan Reid

POETRY PATRONS: SONNET
Marie Baker, Patricia Ferguson, Alan W Gray, Eithne Hand, Neville Keery,
R John McBratney, Joan McBreen, Marian Richardson

POETRY PATRONS: STANZA
Emer Foley, Robert Haughton, Isabel Healy, Monica McInerney, Mary O'Donnell

POETRY PATRONS: HAIKU
Sarah Bannan, Amanda Bell, Peter Clarke, Kevin Conroy, Richard Halperin,
Karen Hanratty, Christine Dwyer Hickey, Mary Jeffrey, John D Kelly, Susie Kennelly,
Oliver Mooney, Jean O'Brien, Gillian Perdue, Andy Pollak, John Prebble, Grace Smith,
Anne Tannam, Siún Tobin, Jesko Zimmerman

Poetry Ireland Review is published three times a year by Poetry Ireland CLG. The Editor
enjoys complete autonomy in the choice of material published. The contents of this
publication should not be taken to reflect either the views or the policy of the publishers.

ISBN: 978-1-902121-79-6   ISSN: 0332-2998

IRISH-LANGUAGE EDITOR: **Caitríona Ní Chléirchín**

PUBLICATIONS MANAGER: **Paul Lenehan** and **Eoin Rogers**, with the assistance of
Maddie Weber and **Orla Higgins**
COVER DESIGN: **Alistair Keady (www.hexhibit.com)**
COVER CREDIT: *Our lives like shadows come and go* (2019), by **Louise Leonard**

Contents   Poetry Ireland Review 130

Colette Bryce	5	EDITORIAL
Zaffar Kunial	7	FOXGLOVE COUNTRY
	8	LITTLE BOOKS
Molly Twomey	10	FIONNUALA
Elizabeth McIntosh	11	THE HAIRCUT
Julie Morrissy	12	THE DEMOCRAT (1944)
Erik Kennedy	14	TO A COUPLE WHO HAD THEIR RINGS BROUGHT TO THE ALTAR BY DRONE AT THEIR GARDEN WEDDING
Michael Longley	15	ET
	16	NEW POEM
	17	BROTHER
Michael Prior	18	ARCADIA
Martina Evans	19	VILE JELLY
	20	SNAKE IN MY SHOE
Michael Martin	21	THE HOURS ARE BANANAS
Susannah Dickey	22	POST MORTEM
	23	SURROUND TOWN
Susan Millar DuMars	24	ST. ANTHONY ACCUSED BY DEVILS
Henri Cole	25	(RE)CREATION
Katherine Duffy	26	LAMENT OF THE VIRUS
Kathryn Simmonds	27	MERCY
Doireann Ní Ghríofa	28	ESSAY: from *A GHOST IN THE THROAT*
Keith Payne	35	INTERVIEW: JOHN KELLY
Máirtín Coilféir	42	AIF SAN IND
Gabriel Rosenstock	43	SIX TANKA TO HER
Cathal Ó Searcaigh	46	'TÁ TÍR FO-THOINN INA SHÚILE …'
	47	'SHÍLFEÁ AGUS MÉ DO MHÓRADH …'
Máire Dinny Wren	48	MEARSCAIPTHE
India Harris	49	REVIEW: JULIE MORRISSY, MARY JEAN CHAN, RACHAEL ALLEN
Eiléan Ní Chuilleanáin	54	REVIEW: DOROTHY MOLLOY
Liam Carson	58	REVIEW: SALLY WEN MAO, FRANNY CHOI
Stiofán Ó Cadhla	62	REVIEW: PADDY BUSHE, MÁIRE DINNY WREN
David Toms	65	REVIEW: CHRISTODOULOS MAKRIS, MATT KIRKHAM, NATASHA CUDDINGTON
Ruth McIlroy	69	TO TRICKY MARGARET, WHO HAD SPREAD A SLANDEROUS ACCOUNT OF THE POETESS
Alan Gillis	70	SCAFFOLDING
	71	DIONYSUS IN BELFAST
Gerard Smyth	72	THE RAIN IN ARMAGH
	73	AMERICAN POETS
Afric McGlinchey	74	HELICO
Rebecca Morgan Frank	75	LIONFISH ROBOT

Liz Quirke	76	GOING TO GROUND
Eleanor Hooker	77	THE CONSOLATIONS OF SILENCE ARE FEW
Greg Delanty	78	HIGH COUP
	79	ON VIEWING *THE ROSES OF HELIOGABALUS*
Emily S Cooper	80	BABIES
Mícheál McCann	81	LEAVING LONDON FOR BELFAST
	82	ÉTUDES
Lorna Shaughnessy	84	ERASURE
Paul Maddern	85	13 FRAGMENTS
Tom French	86	CAST
John Kelly	87	LOCAL KNOWLEDGE
	88	SPACE
Simon Costello	89	THE LANDSLIDE
Sharon Black	90	CAFÉ DES ARTS
	91	HER HAIR
Tara Bergin	92	HOME-SCHOOLING
Nessa O'Mahony	93	REVIEW: PAT BORAN, MOYA CANNON, PATRICK DEELEY
Benjamin Keatinge	98	REVIEW: FRANK ORMSBY, ENDA COYLE-GREENE, PETER SIRR
Nicholas Grene	105	REVIEW: CIARAN CARSON, PAUL MULDOON
Matthew Rice	110	REVIEW: SCOTT MCKENDRY, CAITLIN NEWBY, GRACE WILENTZ, LOUISE G COLE
Helen Meany	115	REVIEW: CATHERINE PHIL MACCARTHY, ENDA WYLEY, MACDARA WOODS
Derek Mahon	120	EVERYTHING IS GOING TO BE ALL RIGHT
Notes on Contributors	121	

Editorial

Settling the text of my first issue has coincided with extraordinary events that seem impossible to ignore in these few words of introduction. Staff at Poetry Ireland, like many people across the island, are working remotely from home, while government advice on social distancing increases in its imperative day by day. In this fast-moving and news-saturated moment, it is hard to predict in which context you, our readers, will be receiving and reading this issue. Thoughts of spring and new phases – both editorial and in the leadership of Poetry Ireland – have been quickly displaced by a sweeping international panic, the fear itself perhaps more contagious than the virus, Covid-19, for which scientists are urgently seeking a vaccine.

Such subjects have challenged poets in the past, and will do so again as this pandemic continues to unfold. IMMA's recent retrospective of Derek Jarman's work reminded us of the art and literature of the AIDS epidemic, a crisis equal in fear but unequalled in the now infamous influence of homophobia and tabloid hysteria in slowing progress on treatment and cure. Alongside the art and activism of Jarman and his peers, poets wrestled with the subject in their lives and in their work: 'My body insisted on restlessness', wrote Thom Gunn in his powerful collection *The Man with the Night Sweats*, 'having been promised love, / as my mind insisted on words / having been promised the imagination. / So I remained alert, confused and uncomforted. / I fared on and, though the landscape did not change, / it came to seem after a while like a place of recuperation' ('A Sketch of the Great Dejection'). In 'The Missing', he conjures a dance of transmission: 'Contact of friend led to another friend, / Supple entwinement through the living mass / Which for all that I knew might have no end, / Image of an unlimited embrace.'

While the concept of self-isolation may be less of a stretch for poets, whose work has always necessitated solitude, it is nonetheless other to the nature of poetry, which is to connect and connect (a tenet central to the work of Poetry Ireland). The mind-mapping impulse inherent to image-making, where one thing links unexpectedly to another, may remind us of molecular patterns of connection, that everything is in everything else. 'Poetry is energy, it is an energy storing and energy releasing device', observed the poet and immunologist Miroslav Holub when interviewed for this magazine many years ago. Dennis O'Driscoll recalled Holub's description to some schoolchildren of poetry as 'a virus transmitted by the poet'. He recounted this in relation to what he saw as the 'immediately infectious' quality of the Czech poet's work, with its intellectual precision and clarity (not to mention humour), an effect paralleled in O'Driscoll's own, with its wry, compassionate gaze. O'Driscoll's poem 'Germ

Warfare' concludes with an address to sneezy fellow passengers, with 'unprotected schnozz': 'thoughts wander back to you, / Eyes water, touched by the largesse with which you showered me, // Smitten to the core by your infectious charms. Bless you!'

To our readers and writers at this uncertain time: stay safe. In Gunn's words, we remain alert, confused and uncomforted. We fare on.

– **Colette Bryce**, 16 March 2020

Zaffar Kunial

FOXGLOVE COUNTRY

Sometimes I like to hide in the word
foxgloves – in the middle of *foxgloves*.
The *xgl* is hard to say, out of the England
of its harbouring word.
Alone it becomes a small tangle,
a witch's thimble, hard-to-toll bell,
elvish door to a door. *Xgl*
a place with a locked beginning
then a snag, a *gl*
like the little Englands of my grief,
a knotted dark that locks light
in *glisten, glow, glint, gleam*
and Oberon's banks of *eglantine*
which closes in on the opening
of *Gulliver* whose shrunken *gul*
says 'rose' in my fatherland.
Meanwhile, in the motherland, the *xg*
is almost the thumb of a lost mitten,
an impossible interior, deeper than forests
and further in. And deeper inland
is the gulp, the gulf, the gap, the grip
that goes before *love*.

Zaffar Kunial

LITTLE BOOKS

> *The universal God of [deletion] might [?]*
> – C. Brontë, little book transcript

I. DEAR

Charlotte, I'm remembering when
I asked you what book was dearest
and best. You answered right. Then
like a collared Lear, I asked: *next best?*
You said, *Father, it is the book of nature.*
Sometimes I can't bear to look, down
to the church. Lately you're inside too.
Sometimes, in grief, a stone is sermon.
An impossible book. Small and seamed:
lives, dates, far lands, stories, crammed
like a wish for more world. For wings.
Unworldly things in a tiny hand. Then
I'll remember your future. Your stone.
And. And. And. And. And. And.

II. THE VERY MINUTE

Six young men wish to let themselves out
[+ ?] hire for the purpose of cleaning out
pocket[s] they are in reduced CirCuMstanCes.
I read *cleaning out* in its helpful sense:
lint, sand, fluff ... Words have pockets.
Small, deep pockets that go on for ages.
We put words on a page and they preserve
infinitely more than we mean or guess. Turn
tiny words like *in* out – even the very *minute*
packs in so much world; we should advertise
to sort out the mess. I see magnified elves
in their *reduced CirCuMstanCes*, holding next
to nothing in such small, small hands, open
like a page of a little book in a museum.

III. HIDER

Bookbinder. The littler. Oldest. Older.
Littling pages for the fingers of a toy
soldier. You carry a title of old Nelson.
The Duke of Bronté. Bronte. Thunder.
Greek god. Island town. Shield-bearer
for Zeus, or Jupiter, the child of Rhea
and Chronos, or Time. And later, after
these little books for the lead soldiers
you'd be Currer Bell. Invisible. Walker
in your new career. Hiding worlds in a
fogdrop. Littler. Speller. Courier. Carer.
The way griefs hide. In letters. Thunder
in foxglove bells. Littler. Than my mum.
Her stoneless grave. Teacher. Carrier on.

Molly Twomey

FIONNUALA

My friends get matching piercings,
sip Smirnoff on roof-top bars,
while I push a double buggy,
cut jam sandwiches into hearts.

Maybe I shouldn't have called
Dad's rebound a hag.
But, God, how she glared at the twins,
stuck a pin in Conn's bum,
spat on Fiachra's rusk.

I was subtle at first,
glued her *Marie Claire* together,
deleted photos of Dad off her iPad,
put her mini on DoneDeal,
convinced her pasta was gluten-free.

But when she caught me
scrubbing Fiachra's potty
with her pink toothbrush,
she said *Goodbye, good luck, I've had enough.*

I didn't hear the wallop she gave the back door,
the curse she hissed under her tongue.
I was shut in the bathroom,
pulling the last of her hair from Mam's brush.

Elizabeth McIntosh

THE HAIRCUT

The wind on the back of the house is cold,
this August more autumn
than summer; rain thumbs the glass.
The house smells sweet and dark, like tea
and I suck in great gulps of air; distant,
wet-nosed Ben Bulben greets a fog from the sea.

In town, I complained about my hair,
now I sit in a towel
and you have gone upstairs
to fetch your father's clippers, leaving me bare-breasted
in the kitchen. *Do you trust me?*
A humourless question.

You put the old blades to my temple, they tug at my skin
and the shorn bit falls like a breeze,
pausing, you ask again.
Jesus, I sigh the way you often do
so the buzz returns, a rough kiss behind my ear
and with your vague language, I have not lied.

Julie Morrissy

THE DEMOCRAT (1944)

the McGees held a unique position
                        like superheroes
with Daddy holding the keys to Waterworks House
the only man in town with a telephone
born after his father died
he had the cure
         for whooping cough
he was the man
who could put out fires
turn on the taps
             make it flow
give life to a village or a child

             Fra didn't lick it off the stones

when she came home with the clipping from *The Democrat*
folded tightly in her purse
meticulous, sharp corners
like how she amassed wrapping paper on Christmas Day
an eco-heroine before her time

Daddy laughed
a sound so convivial
his whole body jerked and tumbled
bemused at his daughter's naivety
her ambition

                 The bearer has been in our employment

                 as secretary for over three years

                 we feel confident she will fill any position of trust

didn't she know they weren't that desperate?
didn't she know
that young women from the South
wouldn't be brought up to the posh offices
of the Great Northern Railway
with the managers, the stationmasters, the clerks

> The bearer was employed as book-keeper
>
> shorthand and typewriting
>
> during which time I found her studious and efficient
>
> trustworthy and honest
>
> she leaves me of her own free will

Fra drew a long breath and smiled
hugged her father
creased and folded the advert
back into her pocket
she stepped away from the kitchen table at Drumnasilla
a slight skip in her step
an unnoticed raised eyebrow

Sept. 13th, 1944
Fra moved to Belfast

she left of her own free will

Erik Kennedy

TO A COUPLE WHO HAD THEIR RINGS BROUGHT TO
THE ALTAR BY DRONE AT THEIR GARDEN WEDDING

I'll say this for you: you're unafraid of mockery
and the coldly irritable judgements of posterity.
You're unafraid of accusations of faddishness.
You're possibly unafraid of technology itself.
And, most impressively, you're unafraid of the wind,
which bucked the drone almost to ringlessness.
It was a katabatic wind that brought a chill
to the wedding party and unnerved the nerveless
among the guests. It was just an everyday wind, really,
a Saturday gust that wouldn't have troubled
a pair of ring-bearing kids dressed like elderly dove-breeders
in their flat caps and braces, or like Arts and Crafts fairies
with acanthus-embroidered cushions and Celtic buttons.
But the drone felt the drama in the wind,
and the drone alone knew how to fit it into
this day that you say is a whole life in miniature.
It's time for the presents. The quadcopter operator
offers the pitch and yaw. The caterers offer the rolls.
The only perfect rhyme for 'lover' is 'lover'.
Go forth and hover.

Michael Longley

ET

It was you who alerted me to *et*
In the love elegies of Propertius,
How it dominates and insinuates,
Separates and joins – an ambiguous word
Et stood for poetry and you and me
Translating from the erotic Latin
'Cupid' and a girlfriend shipwrecked – and death
When my father died and your father died
And we followed Sextus to the black house
And through 'Cornelia', his great death-ode
('May I reach heaven and my ancestors,
My bones conveyed there in the ship of death')
And we took him with us when we married
Enacting that mysterious syllable.

Michael Longley

NEW POEM

I dreamed I had discovered a poem by Catullus,
Its shape projected against my eyelids, its pulse
In my ear, its meaning beginning to emerge.
When I woke I translated it into silence.

Michael Longley

BROTHER

That Catullus line – *multas per gentes* –
Applies to you, my marine engineer
Circumnavigating the globe, and me
Following you in my imagination
Across many a sea to speak in vain
To your ashes. My twin torn from my life,
Accept this elegy wet with my weeping.
Steer your tanker towards eternity –
Greetings, dear sailor, my brother, goodbye.

Michael Prior

ARCADIA

So this is how the sadness comes,
the sight of what won't and can't be undone:
white pines stripped and charred by lightning,
a flicked cigarette blinking
like the pilot light which blossomed red then blue
beneath the hands that held the kettle
and, trembling, filled each glazed cup to the brim.
I still see her. Seeding nothing,
handfuls of ash in a furnace fed by fossil-
branches, bitumen burnt into aerosol,
invisible and catalytic
as the hurt – its search for feeling's older order
in false equivalencies, frayed acrylic
of a red cardigan, once worn and once warm.

Martina Evans

VILE JELLY
– for Julian Calder

Looking at things, really looking at things
is harder, why films might be more scarring
than books except for Macbeth whose knocking
eye-words beat a tattoo in my head at sixteen.
Add to that Gloucester's vile jelly-eye extracted
and wobbling – where? In Cornwall's hand?
Or on the floor and staring up at them all as Regan
hisses, *Let him smell his way to Dover.*
Looking, looking, looking – all my life
trying to get things straight with crooked eyes
that never can line anything up.
White uniform every day for fifteen years,
shifty-eyed in my shining disguise, forced to stare
right into other people's eyes to get their sinuses straight.
That English radiographer who came down in '86 – white
– into the smoky Mater staffroom from ENT theatre
after being eyeballed by a blown-up eye on a TV monitor
during the lunch-time op. Said he'd never liked eyes.
And we were instantly and sympathetically nauseous
in our sandwiches and cigs
because we were used to orthopaedics, yellow bone
and pink muscle, electric saws and bloody swabs.
But a big eye looking at you? That was too new,
a horror like when a bad accident came in
on the ground floor to Casualty, displaying the same
bone and muscle exposed but unexpected under
the torn denim of a leg of jeans. I had to turn
my eyes away,
cover bone and flesh
with whatever I had,
X-ray through any material at all, rather than look at
what was ordinary, two floors up.

Martina Evans

SNAKE IN MY SHOE

It starts on the train home, pins and needles
at first, a numbness spreading until my sole
is lifted, forced up inside my brown shoe.

The flat green fields after Portarlington rush past
the window. We sit facing each other across
the table – May, Mammy, Joan and myself.

I can't feel the floor. I stamp my new club
foot and Mammy gives me a look as the flat head
rears like it will go through me. First time

in Dublin. Tom and his Bank of Ireland friend
met us, a haze through the trees in Phoenix Park,
dusty lion and giraffes standing out

as if they'd been coloured in. In the dead heat of the
suffocating snake house, Tom and John banged fists
on the glass, the air around me collapsing as they

laughed. But I couldn't breathe. The boa constrictor
rose like Lazarus. A pile of yellow and brown
leaves assembled into a tower of rearing muscle,

throwing itself against the glass. I couldn't stop seeing it.
Even after I left the snake house, the zoo. Even now –
in the rackety carriage, the pins and needles build

the balloon of his rage inside the small leather
enclosure of my Clarks' laced-up No.1 size shoe.
He twists and swells.

Michael Martin

THE HOURS ARE BANANAS

      Undertaker, just the thought of you
used to yuck us out.
But we're old now and would love to have you
          here at the party.

      We have ex-ballerinas pirouetting
in the backyard, a kitchen filling up with substitute teachers
who have come to sit on the granite countertops
to bounce their feet to the beat,
grouse about boss and spouse
          and all the rest of it.

We have an astronaut's ex-kid letting a palm
full of spices slip slowly through his
fingers into the giant stewpot,
a dentist recognising her own teeth
in the smile of a long-lost identical
twin while waiting in line for the bathroom.

Were our houses ever really tidy?
Did our shoes ever fit?
          So many weird things happened on our skin.

      O Mortician, your hours must be bananas
and not a single soul to talk to all day.
Drop who you're doing and get on over here.
We're going to crank up the tunes.
We're going to boogie down.
We're going to kill
the lights until nothing remains.

Susannah Dickey

POST MORTEM

Her insides open with the thick vapour of maraschino acid. Her intestines marinade sinister. Bet her uterus looks like an attacked vine tomato we say. Too lilting and neglected. Hocked salsa and old potatoes. Forget it. How sordid is it to invent a reason to put your hands in a woman's insides. Give us some credit. Credit for the fatherly chicken skin on her inner thighs – the parts the fire couldn't mutate. Before she died an enemy fear leapt onto all the different parts of her. Now we're catching it in syllable-shaped silver tins. One man was reluctant to come forward he felt like a crazy man coming and telling a crazy story. A woman's debilitating unbelieved-ness infects everything it touches and it's here on her face along with winter and sabotage and misery and fabulous. How unnecessary it seems to kill a woman like this. So soft and so un-mummed. So fabulous.

Susannah Dickey

SURROUND TOWN

Nothing for days. So fast-forward. Egg timer. Tomato method. Millennium. Count the petticoat fishing boats on the perimeters. They are rampant and innumerable but count them anyway. It's important. Count their cinnamon furies. Draw a big circle on the ground with mountain rescue chalk and find a local man with a metal detector. Listen to the man say *This is a good noise* to his metal detector. Listen to the man say *When you're alone it's a creepy thing* to his metal detector. Notice how the detector's equine neck is like a virgule offering discovery on one side and voluntary redundancy on the other. Choose neither. Send half your crew to the far north and the other half to the local millinery to buy you a flattering and handsome searching hat. Dig up clods of earth and find the blue child's backpack run through with tree roots. Notice how it looks like Medusa's head. *Hard to get any hibernating done with all these damn snakes* it says. Look at the light on the Svartediket. It's nacreous. Look to the sun's aureus disco pants as a way of telling the time. Notice the growing no-light on the cold earth. It's like balsamic. Make a restorative snack before heading back to the lab. Tie a pink ribbon around the houses so as not to alarm the people. Let their excitement die. Let their amicable chat wither. Isdal remains Isdal. Plug the holes in your head with wet sheets to keep the spiders out.

Susan Millar DuMars

ST. ANTHONY ACCUSED BY DEVILS
after Hieronymus Bosch

He looks different from this distance,
my brother.
His head is that of a curlew,
white throated, quick eyed.
Yet he doesn't fly
but skates across the river
a list of my crimes
skewered on his beak.

The Devil is a poet –
metaphor master.
This frozen river,
my beak and claw brother,
slow and silent,
bearing my indictment –
this is my perdition.
Yours will look different.
The Devil is an artist.
He finds the right image.

Henri Cole

(RE)CREATION

Preferring the company of nature to man,
disappointed in love, he retreated to the desert.
But this was not any ordinary desert,
for helicopters and jets appeared overhead. A parade of camels.
When a lion came out of the darkness,
the man was angry at his horse for not warning him.
Faraway, it was difficult to see the minarets in a steep-sided valley.
When the Taliban seized him,
they put a noose around his neck,
and he messed his pants.
Faraway, a flute played, a missile launched,
and a child kneeled drinking before a well.
Still, whatever the faults of life,
the merriment of it was only partially erased
by the curious flies of Allah investigating
the carrion hanging in the public square.
It was as if this had not once been a man at all,
but instead a white-winged dove,
its solitary neck and breast washed lightly with pink.
Flocks of these doves are a common sight in summer,
nesting in fragile platforms of twigs,
eating small seeds from the desert willow.
On take-off, they produce, with their wings,
a subtle, unearthly whistle.

Katherine Duffy

LAMENT OF THE VIRUS

Your eye at the microscope
and never a welcome
though we are sculptors
no one will come to our shows
unsung though we strive
flicker under your
We wade your rivers
bask in the stinking
your elaborate heart
your intricate ear
we tattoo on your brain
Diligent and faithful we are
children the old ones
Only consider
our incomparable crowns
fill the air the sea
wipe the world
but your eye
so cold

always so cold
though we visit and visit and
of masterful writhing
Our feats of aviation go
through the air to reach you
eyelid when you look away
doze in your hollows
steam of your organs
our dancehall
palace and labyrinth
our shamanic dreams
fond we love animals
We are so light to carry
our entrancing shapes
our superlative efforts
We seethe and sigh
polish the bones
at the microscope always

Kathryn Simmonds

MERCY

Whatever may ravage us tomorrow
has not come today,
and so my children are still young,
my body is their tree
and we have no safe distances.

Sleeve to sleeve I peg out shirts.
White sky, if you won't promise anything,
why should I complain?

Doireann Ní Ghríofa

FROM *A GHOST IN THE THROAT*

> *We are an echo that runs, skittering,*
> *through a train of rooms.*
> — Czesław Miłosz

When we first met, I was a child, and she had been dead for centuries.

Look: I am eleven, a girl who is terrible at sums and at sports, a girl given to staring out windows, a girl whose only real gift lies in daydreaming. The teacher snaps my name, startling me back to the flimsy prefab. Her voice makes it a fine day in 1773, and sets English soldiers crouching in ambush. I add ditch-water to drench their knees. Their muskets point towards a young man who is tumbling from his saddle now, in slow, slow motion. A woman rides in to kneel over him, her voice rising in an antique formula of breath and syllable the teacher calls a 'caoineadh', a keen to lament the dead. Her voice generates an echo strong enough to reach a girl in the distance with dark hair and bitten nails. Me.

In the classroom, we are presented with an image of this woman standing alone, a convenient breeze setting her as a windswept, rosy-cheeked colleen. This, we are told, is Eibhlín Dubh Ní Chonaill, among the last noblewomen of the old Irish order. Her story seems sad, yes, but also a little dull. Schoolwork. Boring. My gaze has already soared away with the crows, while my mind loops back to my most-hated pop song, 'and you give yourself away …' No matter how I try to oust them, those lyrics won't let me be.

~

By the time I find her again, I only half-remember our first meeting. As a teenager I develop a schoolgirl crush on this *caoineadh*, swooning over the tragic romance embedded in its lines. When Eibhlín Dubh describes falling in love at first sight and abandoning her family to marry a stranger, I love her for it, just as every teenage girl loves the story of running away forever. When she finds her murdered lover and drinks handfuls of his blood, I scribble pierced hearts in the margin. Although I don't understand it yet, something ricochets in me whenever I return to this image of a woman kneeling to drink from the body of a lover, something that reminds me of the inner glint I feel whenever a boyfriend presses his teenage hips to mine and his lips to my throat.

My homework is returned to me with a large red X, and worse, the teacher's scrawl cautions: 'Don't let your imagination run away with you!' I have felt these verses so deeply that I know my answer must be correct, and so, in righteous exasperation, I thump page after page down hard as I make my way back to the poem, scowling. In response to the request 'Describe the poet's first encounter with Art Ó Laoghaire', I had written: 'She jumps on his horse and rides away with him forever', but on returning, I am baffled to find that the teacher is correct: this image does not exist in the text. If not from the poem, then where did it come from? I can visualise it so clearly: Eibhlín Dubh's arms circling her lover's waist, her fingers woven over his warm belly, the drumming of hooves, and the long ribbon of hair streaming behind her. It may not be real to my teacher, but it is to me.

~

If my childhood understanding of this poem was, well, childish, and my teenage interpretation little more than a swoon, my readings swerved again in adulthood.

I had no classes to attend anymore, no textbooks or poems to study, but I had set myself a new curriculum to master. In attempting to raise our family on a single income, I was teaching myself to live by the rigours of frugality. I examined classified ads and supermarket deals with care. I met internet strangers and handed them coins in exchange for bundles of their babies' clothes. I sold bundles of our own. I roamed car boot sales, haggling over toddler toys and stair-gates. I only bought car seats on sale. There was a doggedness to be learned from such thrift, and I soon took to it.

My earliest years of motherhood, in all their fatigue and awe and fretfulness, took place in various rented rooms of the inner city. Although I had been raised in the countryside, I found that I adored it there: the terraces of smiling neighbours with all their tabbies and terriers, all our bins lined up side by side, the overheard cries of rage or lust in the dark, and the weekend parties with their happy, drunken choruses. Our taps always dripped, there were rats in the tiny yard, and the night city's glimmering made stars invisible, but when I woke to feed my first son, and then my second, I could split the curtains and see the moon between the spires. In those city rooms, I wrote a poem. I wrote another. I wrote a book. If the poems that came to me on those nights might be considered love poems, then they were in love with rain and alpine flowers, with the strange vocabularies of a pregnant body, with clouds and with grandmothers. No poem arrived in praise of the man who slept next to me as I wrote, the man whose moonlit skin always drew my lips towards him. The love I held for him felt too vast to pour into the neat vessel of a poem. I couldn't put it into words. I still can't. As he dreamt, I watched poems hurrying towards me through the dark. The city had lit something in me, something that pulsed, vulnerable as a fontanelle, something that trembled, as I did, between bliss and exhaustion.

We had already moved house twice in three years, and still the headlines reported that rents were increasing. Our landlords always saw opportunity in such bulletins, and who could blame them? Me. I blamed them every time we were evicted with a shrug. No matter how glowing their letters of reference, I always resented being forced to leave another home. Now we were on the cusp of moving again. I'd searched for weeks, until eventually I found a nearby town with lower rents. We signed another lease, packed our car, and left the city. I didn't want to go. I drove slow, my elbow straining to change gear, wedged between our old TV and a bin-bag of teddies, my voice leading a chorus through "five little ducks went swimming one day". I found my way along unfamiliar roads, "over the hills and far away", scanning signs for Bishopstown and Bandon, for Macroom and Blarney, while singing "Mammy Duck said Quack, Quack, Quack ..." until my eye tripped over a sign for Kilcrea.

Kilcrea – Kilcrea – the word repeated in my mind as I unlocked a new door, it repeated and repeated as I scoured dirt from the tiles, and grimaced at the biography of old blood and semen stains on the mattresses. *Kilcrea, Kilcrea*, the word vexed me for days, as I unpacked books and coats and baby monitors, spoons and towels and tangled phone chargers, until finally, I remembered – *Yes!* – in that old poem from school, wasn't Kilcrea the name of the graveyard where the poet buried her lover? I cringed, remembering my crush on that poem, as I cringed when I recalled all the skinny rock stars torn and tacked onto my teenage walls, the vocabulary they allowed me to express the beginnings of desire. I flinched, in general, at my teenage self. She made me uncomfortable, that girl, how she displayed her wants so brashly, that girl who flaunted a schoolbag Tipp-Exed with longing, who scribbled her own marker over layers of laneway graffiti, who stared obscenely at strangers from bus windows, who met their eyes and held them until she saw her own lust stir there. The girl caught in forbidden behaviours behind the school and threatened with expulsion. The girl called a *slut* and a *whore* and a *frigid bitch*. The girl condemned to 'silent treatment'. The girl punished and punished and punished again. The girl who didn't care. I was here, singing to a child while scrubbing old shit from a stranger's toilet. Where was she?

~

In the school car park, I found myself a little early to pick up my eldest and sought shelter from the rain under a tree. My son was still dreaming under his plastic buggy-cover, and I couldn't help but admire his ruby cheeks and the plump, dimpled arms I tucked back under his blanket. *There*. In the scrubby grass that bordered the concrete, bumblebees were browsing – if I had a garden of my own, I thought, I'd fill it with low forests of clover and all the ugly weeds they adore, I'd throw myself to my knees in service to bees. I looked past them towards the hills in the distance, and, thinking of that road-sign again, I rummaged for my phone. There were many more verses to the *Caoineadh* than I recalled, thirty, or more.

The poem's landscape came to life as I read, it was alive all around me, alive and fizzing with rain, and I felt myself alive in it. Under that drenched tree, I found her sons, 'Conchubhar beag an cheana is Fear Ó Laoghaire, an leanbh' – which I translated to myself as 'our dotey little Conchubhar / and Fear Ó Laoghaire, the babba'. I was startled to find Eibhlín Dubh pregnant again with her third child, just as I was. I had never imagined her as a mother in any of my previous readings, or perhaps I had simply ignored that part of her identity, since the collision of mother and desire wouldn't have fitted with how my teenage self wanted to see her. As my fingertip-scar navigated the text now, however, I could almost imagine her lullaby-hum in the dark. I scrolled the text from beginning to end, then swiped back to read it all again. Slower, this time.

The poem began within Eibhlín Dubh's gaze as she watched a man stroll across a market. His name was Art and, as he walked, she wanted him. Once they eloped, they led a life that could only be described as opulent: oh, the lavish bedchambers, oh, the delectable meals, oh, the couture, oh, the long, long mornings of sleep in sumptuous duck-down. As Art's wife, she wanted for nothing. I envied her her home and wondered how many servants it took to keep it all going, how many shadow-women doing their shadow-work, the kind of shadow-women I come from. Eibhlín dedicates entire verses to her lover in descriptions so vivid that they shudder with a deep love and a desire that still feels electric, but the fact that this poem was composed after his murder means that grief casts its murk-shadow over every line of praise. How powerful such a cataloguing must have felt in the aftermath of his murder, when each spoken detail conjured him back again, alive and impeccably dressed, with a shining pin glistening in his hat, and 'the suit of fine couture / stitched and spun abroad for you'. She shows us Art as desired, not only by herself, but by others, too, by posh city women who –

> always
> stooped their curtsies low for you.
> How well, they could see
> what a hearty bed-mate you'd be,
> what a man to share a saddle with,
> what a man to spark a child with.

Although the couple were living through the regime of fear and cruelty inflicted by the Penal Laws, her husband was defiant. Despite his many enemies, Art seemed somehow unassailable to Eibhlín, until the day that 'she came to me, your steed, / with her reins trailing the cobbles, / and your heart's blood smeared from cheek to saddle'. In this terrifying moment, Eibhlín neither hesitated nor sought help. Instead, she leapt into that drenched saddle and let her husband's horse carry her to his body. In anguish and in grief, then, she fell upon him, keening and drinking mouthfuls of his blood. Even in such a moment of raw horror, desire remained – she roared over his corpse, ordering him to rise from the dead so she might 'have a bed dressed / in bright blankets / and embellished quilts / to spark your sweat and set it spilling'. But Art was dead, and the text she composed became an evolving record of praise, sorrow, lust, and reminiscence.

Through the darkness of grief, this rage is a lucifer match, struck and sparking. She curses the man who ordered Art's murder: 'Morris, you runt; on you, I wish anguish! – / May bad blood spurt from your heart and your liver! / Your eyes grow glaucoma! / Your knee-bones both shatter!' Such furies burn and dissipate and burn again, for this is a poem fuelled by the twin fires of anger and desire. Eibhlín rails against all involved in Art's betrayal, including her own brother-in-law, 'that shit-talking clown'. Rage. Rage and anguish. Rage and anguish and love. She despairs for her two young sons, 'and the third, still within me, / I fear will never breathe'. What losses this woman has suffered. What losses are yet to come. She is in pain, as is the poem itself; this text is a text in pain. It aches. When the school-bell rang, my son found me in the rain, my face turned towards the hills where Eibhlín Dubh once lived.

That night, the baby squirmed inside me until I abandoned sleep, scrambling for my phone instead. My husband instinctively curled his sleeping body into mine; despite his snores, I felt him grow hard against the dip of my back. I frowned, holding very still until I was sure he was asleep, then inching away to whisper the poem to myself, conjuring a voice through hundreds of years, from her pregnant body to mine. As everyone else dreamed, my eyes were open in the dark.

~

Months passed the way months will, in a spin of grocery lists, vomiting bugs, Easter eggs, hoovering, and electricity bills. I grew and grew, until one morphine-bright day in July my third son made his slow way from my belly to my chest, and I found myself in the whip exhaustion of night-feeds again.

Throughout those yellow-nappy weeks, when everything spun wildly in the erratic orbit of others' needs, only the lines of the *Caoineadh* remained steadfast. I kept it under my pillow, and whenever I stirred to feed the baby, Eibhlín Dubh's words broke through my trippy, exhausted haze. Her life and her desires were so distant from mine, and yet she felt so close. Before long, the poem began to leak into my days. My curiosity grew until it sent me out of the house and towards the only rooms that could help.

~

Look: it is a Tuesday morning, and a security guard in a creased blue uniform is unlocking a door and standing aside with a light-hearted bow, because here I come, with my hair scraped into a rough bun, a milk-stained blouse, a baby in a sling, a toddler in a buggy, a nappy-bag spewing books, and what could only be described as a dangerous light in my eyes. I know that I have a six-minute window at best before the screeching begins, so I am unclipping the buggy, fast, faster now, and urging the toddler upstairs. "No stopping." I peek into the sling where tiny eyelids swipe in sleep, plonk the toddler by my feet and – eyes darting around in search of the librarian who once chastised me – I shove a forbidden banana into his fist. "Please," I whisper, "please, just sit still while Mammy just – just –?"

I tug a wrinkled list from the nappy-bag, my fingertips racing the spines. *Just two minutes*, I think, *just two*. The sling squirms and the baby rips an extravagant blast into his nappy. I smile (how could I not?), and yank the last two books from the shelf. I am grinning as I kiss the toddler's hair, grinning as I hoist my load sideways, step by slow step down the stairs, with one gooey banana-hand in mine, and a very familiar smell rising from the sling.

This is how a woman in my situation comes to chase down every translation of Eibhlín Dubh's words, of which there are many, necessitating many such library visits. Such is the number of individuals who have chosen to translate this poem that it seems almost like a rite of passage, or a series of cover-versions of a beloved old song. Many of the translations I find feeble – dead texts that try, but fail, to find the thumping pulse of Eibhlín Dubh's presence – but some are memorably strong. Few come close enough to her voice to satiate me, and the accompanying pages of her broader circumstances are often so sparse that they leave me hungry. Not just hungry. I am starving. I long to know more of her life, both before and after the moment of composition. I want to know who she was, where she came from, and what happened next. I want to know what became of her children and grandchildren. I want to read details of her burial place so I can lay flowers on her grave. I want to know her, and to know her life, and I am lazy, so I want to find all these answers laid out easily before me, preferably in a single library book. The literature available to me, however, is mostly uninterested in answering such peripheral curiosities. Still, I search, because I am convinced that there must be a text in existence, somewhere, that shares my wonder.

Once I exhaust the public libraries, I set to asking favours of university friends, stealing into libraries under assumed identities to make stealth-copies of various histories, volumes on translation, and journal articles, each source adding a brushstroke or two to the portrait of Eibhlín Dubh that is growing in my mind. I use them to add new words to my stashes of information, tucking copies under our bed, in the car, and by the breast-pump. My weeks are decanted between the twin forces of milk and text, weeks that soon pour into months, and then into years. I make myself a life in which whenever I let myself sit, it is to emit pale syllables of milk, while sipping my own dark sustenance from ink.

~

A Ghost in the Throat *will be published by Tramp Press later this year: 'A portrait of a poet drawing a portrait of a poet, it is not only a stitching of two women's days, it is a sleuthing.'*

With thanks to Doireann Ní Ghríofa and her publisher, Tramp Press (**www.tramppress.com**), for permission to include this excerpt from A Ghost in the Throat.

IN CONVERSATION: KEITH PAYNE TALKS TO POET JOHN KELLY

Keith Payne: I've been listening to John Kelly on the radio long enough to recognise his voice: the soft Fermanagh phrase, the underplayed wit. That voice has aired my rooms from a bedsit by the Grand Canal to a shed on Inis Mór to an unearthly hot Sydney suburb with the kookaburras laughing outside along the telephone wires. And when I pick up Kelly's *Notions*, published by Dedalus Press in 2018 and shortlisted for both the 2019 Shine/Strong award and the inaugural Farmgate Café National Poetry Award, that voice is immediately recognizable: the 'Northern southpaw, / leading with the right – / addressing the thing.'

I met John Kelly in Books Upstairs last year, on a cold January morning with the Dublin seagulls skirling over D'Olier Street. On the shelf behind him is an early novel of his that was compared to Flann O'Brien: "But I hadn't read O'Brien by the time that novel came out. That's just how we spoke where I come from." So much has been said about the poet's voice, from the sounds heard behind the door to the words simply 'having the feel of you about them'. The best way to hear the voice is of course to simply sit and read the poems, or, as is the case now, to sit and transcribe an interview with the poet, attentive to every word.

KP: *Notions* has been well received so far, there's already been some good reviews.

John Kelly: You know, there are friends of mine who don't know I ever wrote, because it was another lifetime, it was another place. It was basically university and immediately after university, and for most of us that's a whole other lifetime and a whole other world. We've moved into another arena, and people have no idea what you were doing when you were at university, which is just as well actually.

KP: And did you stop writing after you graduated?

JK: No, not entirely. The shorthand of it is there were a bunch of us at Queen's who were writing – student poets, same as everywhere else. We'd go to a group that Medbh McGuckian ran once a week and read stuff. There was no vicious criticism going on, but it was encouraging all the same, and then we would read at student events or maybe as a support act to a visiting poet. People would come through like Sorley MacLean, and Paul Durcan would have read there a few times. And then of course the Northern Irish poets would be knocking around: Frank Ormsby, James Simmons, Michael Longley obviously, and John Hewitt was still knocking around. And I knew some of the older ones like Roy McFadden, who I would have made a point of visiting.

KP: Was Muldoon an influence back then as he is now on the young poets in the North?

JK: For a start, back when I was a student, I wouldn't have understood it, frankly, my lack of references and so on. The only poems I would have known, really well, would have been ones like 'Duffy's Circus', the earlier, shorter poems, you know. 'Why Brownlee Left' and those sorts of things, I loved those. By the time I started working at the BBC, Muldoon was gone – I might even have taken over his office, but he wasn't present in Belfast back then.

KP: By the look of some of those early poems though, you were reading a lot of Montague?

JK: Early on I came across his books in a shop in Enniskillen called Halls, and they had a surprisingly great poetry collection, and I would have read Montague standing at the back of the shop. I read *The Rough Field* and any poems of his that had been anthologised. I only met John much later in life, and funnily enough we hit it off. I always assumed he was a severe, distant, sharp character, but I was missing the mischief, then when I met him, obviously I realised there was a twinkle in his eye and I got really fond of him. There were poets who were around and you'd see them every day, and there were poets who had left. I kind of envied those ones. Mahon was gone and of course Seamus too. I couldn't but envy him the idea that he was in Wicklow.

KP: So there was a sense that those poets had managed to escape, that they had gotten out while you were still in the same place?

JK: Well, yes. He had made it beyond that circle, a circle that felt to me like it was getting ever smaller, and I was at an age where I didn't want that. You're deeply honoured to be included in the company, but you get to a point when the idea of walking down Sandymount Strand seemed a whole lot more attractive than walking down Botanic Avenue, at that particular time. Because don't forget it was Belfast in the Eighties. It wasn't a nice place and we were living in an ever-decreasing area while there was a bigger world out there.

I wasn't from Belfast so I never felt entirely comfortable there anyway. I lingered for work reasons, but I always wanted to move out. And when it got to the point when we bunch of poets should be stepping up to the mark and producing something, I felt as if I wasn't getting anywhere, and all of a sudden I just kinda got sick of the scene.

I started to very deeply mistrust what I was doing and why I was doing it, and at that age – I shouldn't beat myself up too much about it – I was starting to doubt my motives or doubt the purity of the thing. I had a facility for wordplay and jokes and all that stuff, so I'd get a laugh. I was funny, so then I was responding to that, and factoring in things like timing, so I started to think: Hold on, what am I now? I'm a stand-up comedian, that's what I am; I'm not writing poetry. So, one night I was giving a reading and I just went out and delivered the poems with no introduction or anything: 1-2-3-4-5, then I got off the stage and that was that, I just knocked it on the head.

KP: And you never wrote again?

JK: I was writing prose and trying to rely on the language as you can with poetry, and that didn't work. The prose I liked was more about language than plot or character, and I thought the language would carry it through. I had mixed results. And the years passed, very fast, and the next thing I knew I was fifty and you realise everything has changed and it's not like university where you'd try anything once because you suddenly realise you don't have all the time in the world, so you get back to what you're about. It's a combination of that gunk that comes with hitting fifty: married, kids, parents dying, big stuff happening, and in those circumstances I happened to find things coming through. Triggers. I can stand over the book, and I know it has come from a good place; it's honest. A poem written when I was twenty-one was unfinished, whereas I can finish them now.

KP: That reminds me of the radio programme you did with Michael Heaney about Seamus as a teacher. There were archive recordings from Harvard where he's asked if there are any poets among his creative writing students, to which he replied there were two or three who 'had the staying power'.

JK: Staying power is the toughest thing of all. Seamus was very wise, he'd manage to run you through the scanner quite quick and have you sussed. He was kind to me quite early on. Like Dennis O' Driscoll, he would send out the cards, and the line that sticks and is so relevant to me now is from a card he sent me on the publication of an anthology: 'trust them, says I, and trust yourself', which of course is what I didn't do, but I'm doing it now.

KP: And so, you'd tried prose as poetry, but what about the idea that poetry is simply storytelling in its own particular shape? Your collection could be read as a poetic *Bildungsroman* that charts your move from Enniskillen to Belfast, on across the Atlantic to New York, till finally home again and the start of your own family.

JK: Isn't that just everybody's story? I haven't created a story.

KP: But poetry can tell that story.

JK: Oh absolutely it can, yes. I was messing around with something recently to see if I could tell an invented story in poetry, and I'm struggling with that because I don't trust the prose poem when I do it myself. I look at it and go, sure what's that? If someone else does it and hands it to me I go this is great, but if I do it myself I'm not sure. But at least if a poem's not working you discover it more quickly than a novel that's not working.

KP: Or as James Baldwin put it, 'You never get the book you wanted, you settle for the book you get.'

JK: Yeah, but I much prefer the experience of bringing out a poetry book. I've learned a lot from it. I've learned a lot from Pat Boran's comments, and from those people who read the book in advance. It's a generous world, the poetry world.

KP: And your poems are definitely not zeitgeisty, which is good.

JK: I don't know what the zeitgeist is, but I see a type of poetry being published nowadays by the big presses, and it doesn't impress me at all. And I want to be impressed. I want it to be memorable; I want to read lines where I go, 'I wish I'd thought of that.' At the minute I'm reading Ted Kooser. He's old fashioned and I love it. He makes you think you could do it, that there seems to be no great mystery to what he's doing, and that's encouraging. You don't get upset just because you can't do what the greats do. Everyone is blessed in some different way. I was reading something recently about pike, and of course you think of Hughes. But I'm from Fermanagh; I've also got rights on the pike.

KP: Do you think there's a particular northern cant to be heard, like a northern spake, that's sharp and ratcheted up like a rivet going in on the Belfast shipyards?

JK: Well, there could be, yet how they speak in Belfast is completely different to the way we spoke in Enniskillen. We're closer to Donegal and

Monaghan, so it's softer. I know lots of people that I grew up with, and if I was to have a conversation with them now and Muldoon was sitting there, it'd fit in to that kind of of carry-on of picking up a word and running with it. And I think that surely some of that influence seeps through from the place you came from – because everything you read and everything you hear is in there, and whether you know it or not it's working on you somehow, you mightn't even know what you know. For me it was the kind of sense of humour we developed which was twisted and surreal and black. The language is already on its head, it's already twisted, it's already a version of something else. Obviously, this is not news, but a lot of it is a version of Irish spoken in English.

KP: Berger writes about that, what lies behind the text before it was written, the 'inarticulate as well as the articulate'.

JK: Yeah. Sometimes I wish I had just recorded normal conversations of my mother talking just to actually look at the syntax and the way it stands. It's so hugely complex. We had a facility with language, I'm sure everybody has. But the language we were speaking, the words that were flying about in our heads, were rich. It's all that stuff that's going on in the background that creates the magical aspect of writing a poem. You know, sometimes the best things can happen when you're being inattentive.

People like Dylan, Tom Paulin, they can go up into their intellect. Every single experience is accessible to them. They can go up and grab these things at will; they've got this incredible brain. Dylan was at an after-party in Tommy Makem's pub in New York – of course, he's there as opposed to at the official party – and at the end, they'd all been singing and Dylan had been standing there the whole time with the hood up and Tommy says, "Here Bob, sing us a song" and Dylan took the guitar and sang 'Roddy McCorley' word for word, note for note and that was it. How many years had it been since he'd sung that song, if ever? He just knows it, but the rest of us just hit on those things now and then, and that's when we find the magic.

KP: So would you say we're just telling our own story and it works best when we're telling it to ourselves?

JK: That's what I'm talking about with Ted Kooser. It's everyday stuff, but it's not boring. So yes, I think you are, you're talking to yourself and I think that's why after all these years I've done something of consequence for myself. You're not playing to the gallery. I'm older now, I'm not trying to impress anybody, which is a posture, an affectation, and it eventually becomes dishonest. And so you realise there's more to it. It's unnerving to be called a poet now, I'm a bit uneasy about it. There's a difference in writing poems and being a poet, to paraphrase Liam O'Flynn. At the moment I'm writing a lot since the book is out and people are talking about it. I'll probably write something tonight after talking to you, I almost feel like the poems are queuing up, are orbiting to be pulled down.

KP: The poem 'Ornithology' ends with the line of you getting the first and proper sign 'that wondrous things might exist in a life like mine'. Do you think you knew that back then, or did you only realise it when you wrote the poems?

JK: I got it to some extent back then watching nature programmes on TV, or reading the *Ladybird Book of Birds*, and you realise that the thing in the book is in fact there in the garden. When you're growing up and everything is ordinary and ordinariness is being encouraged, the fact that some exoticism you knew from the telly existed in your own garden was a bit of a revelation. I remember going fishing and seeing the great crested grebes, or a kingfisher, or a dragonfly, or the first time I saw a hawk. All this stuff existed on the housing estate where I lived. When I come along the Dart line now, I see the egrets, when I was a kid the only place you saw them was in Tarzan movies.

KP: Yes, there are a lot of birds skirring through the collection. So much so, you could have called it *For the Birds*, if the title wasn't already taken.

JK: Well, there could have been more actually, at one point I thought of calling it *Ornithology*, but it's too grandiose a word.

KP: I've never heard you talk about birds on the radio.

JK: The birds keep coming back, they're there all the time. There will be more in the next book. They're a constant presence and they can mean different things. You know that Heaney line 'I never liked yon bird,' you know that's a tough one. I read that poem and got a real shiver.

KP: The poems in the collection are nicely woven together; they're all pulling on various threads into a rare though recognizable weave.

JK: Well that's where I've to give a lot of credit to Pat Boran, because he organised the book.

KP: You can see there's a strong hand there all right. Did he push against you; did you find yourself resisting his editorial hand on the poems?

JK: No. I have to say that I had enough maturity at my age and common sense to yield to his better judgement. There were poems rejected and I said OK; poems held over because they didn't quite fit; and others where I'd say I'm not sure but he'd say yes. I was happy to get a steer. All you want is for someone to tell you, 'It really is a poem.'

I don't know what it is or why I do it. It's laying down something, a commemoration of something. You do it because it's niggling at you. I wrote most of this stuff in secrecy, no one knew about it apart from the couple of readers. When I was writing the poems, I wasn't thinking of a book. I was writing about normal things. I was upset because my mother had died. I love my children. There's nothing I've said that not everybody else feels. So, anything I say in the poems, I'd say to a total stranger. Was I completely derailed by the death of my father? Yes I was, in ways I never saw coming. But if I say that to any of my friends they'll say, "That's exactly how I felt." As a pal the other day said, "I hardly spoke to my father, but when he died I was lost."

KP: Just like Hartnett's 'I loved her from the day she died.'

JK: It's not therapy, but it steadies you, as Seamus said. And when you've written it, and it's the right shape you've preserved, you've clarified it. You've put it in a better place as opposed to it running randomly around inside your head.

KP: As opposed to your preoccupations running round the washing machine?

JK: Exactly. You take them out and put them in the dryer, you hang them on the line, let the sun shine through them, take them down, fold them, and put them in the hot press.

Máirtín Coilféir

AIF SAN IND

Samhlaím anois thú
– théis dhuit bean mhaith
a dhéanamh dhíot fhéin
Ón tír sin i gcéin ar an bhfón –
Sea, samhlaím thú,
(Mar a déarfá féin)
Ag margántaíocht,
Ag beartaíocht,
Ag stangaireacht leat,
An dúchas sin a bhris
Glan amach tríot – an banfhile
Bán ag aonach na ndonn
Is anois samhlaím liom thú
Sa mbaile sin nach bhfacas
Ag méaráil stór cadáis
Is do bheartsa línéadaigh.

Gabriel Rosenstock

SIX TANKA TO HER

ní liom féin atáim
na géanna fiáine leis ag éamh
tá dúil ag na clocha ionat fiú
      mo dhála féin,
         a thaisce, tráth dá rabhas im' chloch

I am not alone –
wild geese are also crying,
the stones want You too
      the same as I did myself,
         my love, when I was a stone

beidh cuma na hainnise ar ball orthu
giúiseanna sléibhe
ní stopfaidh sé sin an t-éan
      a thagann chun scíth a ligean
         ionatsa mo scíth, a shearc shíor-óg

they'll soon seem wretched,
those pines out on the mountains –
it won't stop the bird
      coming to rest its worn wings –
         in You, ever-young, I rest

éadaí á ní san abhainn ...
a ansacht, glantar gach smaoineamh
gach cuimhne
      ná bíodh ann ach Tusa
      chun na habhann le dras na haigne

clothes washed in the flow –
dear one, clear away all thought,
every memory,
      till there's nothing left but You
      as mind's dross floats downriver

is iomaí speiceas a bhí ionam
is mé ag foghlaim
conas feitheamh leat
      ar aithin tú mé i gcaitheamh na mblianta
      an aithníonn tú anois mé

so many species
I have been, always learning
how to wait for You –
      did You see me down the years,
      do You recognise me now?

anois is ár rún ar eolas acu
baineann na réaltaí bláth dá chéile
ní cuimhin le haon neach beo
      ar feadh soicind fiú
        an chuma a bhí orthu tráth

knowing our secret,
blooming stars eclipse themselves –
no one remembers,
      not even for a second,
        how they appeared in the past

iompaíonn samhradh ina fhómhar
cén uair a tharlaíonn sé sin
cén nóiméad, cén soicind
      taoise dall ar athruithe
        a ghile, ag soilsiú de shíor!

summer births autumn –
but really, when does it change?
what minute, second?
      You – impervious to change –
        bright one, shining forever!

                – translated by **Michael Begnal**

Cathal Ó Searcaigh

'TÁ TÍR FO-THOINN INA SHÚILE ...'

Tá tír fo-thoinn ina shúile, aigéan dúghorm
domhain ina smaointe, teangacha glasa na trá
ina chuid cainte, suaitheadh na dtonn ag borradh
i ngile a gháire is i bhfarraigí arda a ghrá.

Agus amanta tig fronta te ag séideadh isteach
ó mhórmhuir a mhianta, spraisteacha geala a anála
ag éirí go deas i gcamas a bhéil agus i mbruth
a bhriathra agus nuair a éiríonn sé chugam ina ghála,

Ó dhá ros scoite a chos, an tuile ina chúr
geal cuthaigh ag líonadh inbhear a dhúile,
sin an uair a dtig an t-oibriú pléisiúrtha seo
i mo chéadfaí is téim sa tsáile de léim buile.

Cathal Ó Searcaigh

'SHÍLFEÁ AGUS MÉ DO MHÓRADH ...'

Shílfeá agus mé do mhóradh, a chroí, nár lonnaigh mo shúile
ar na huafáis: ar na millliúin a creachadh in ár
na Síre, ar chnámharlaigh an ocrais in Éimin, ar dhíothú
na Rohinga, ar dhiabhalsmacht Isis, ar a bhfuil leagtha acu ar lár

d'oidhreacht an duine, ar dhídeanaí ag tabhairt faoi fharraigí
míthrócraireacha na Meánmhara, ar bhaothghlóir an rachmais,
ar dhaorbhroid an chiníochais, ar a bhfuil feicthe agam, a chroí,
d'aighnis teaghlaigh, de dhéanamh díoltais,de lucht an mhioscais.

Ach a chuid bheag den tsaol, deirim seo leat glan ó mo chroí,
nach bhfuil mairg ná méala, nach bhfuil doilíos ná dólás
nach dtéann go beo ionam óir is tusa mo Rohingeach ag éalú
ón ár, mo Shíreach ar fán gan dídean is m'Éimineach óg gan dóchas.

Máire Dinny Wren

MEARSCAIPTHE

Mhúscail sí as tromluí,

Eagla a craicinn uirthi;

An ag brionglóidí a bhí sí,

Rámhaille na hoíche nó a mhacasamhail?

Scéin ina súile ag scáthánú na scéine sa tír, sa domhan.

Caidé a dhéanfadh sí inniu?

An teach mar phríosún aici agus

Iarsmaí an tseansaoil ag cur eolchaire uirthi.

Phill sí ar an leaba,

Thoiligh sí go léifeadh sí, le héalú tamall.

Húradh ar an raidió go raibh vacsaín ar an bhealach ach bhí

Eangach an ghalair ag teannadh achan lá.

Nóta: húradh = dúradh

India Harris

DEBUT TRIPTYCH

Julie Morrissy, *Where, the Mile End* (tall-lighthouse / Book*hug, 2019), €12 / £12.
Mary Jean Chan, *Flèche* (Faber and Faber, 2019), £10.99.
Rachael Allen, *Kingdomland* (Faber and Faber, 2019), £10.99.

Opening on the wintry shore of Dublin Bay, 'Steel Skin' – the first poem in Julie Morrissy's *Where, the Mile End* – moves associatively from Bull Island to an icy North America, setting in motion the global criss-crossings that characterise this debut collection. Morrissy has biographically 'moved up and down and over', living in Ireland, the US, and Canada, and her poems document these shifting locations. Morrissy has received a Next Generation Artist Award from the Arts Council, and in 2016 was featured in the 'Rising Generation' issue of *Poetry Ireland Review*. In an impressive first collection, what strikes me most about Julie Morrissy is how few writers she reminds me of; in her weaving of Irish and American poetic traditions, she has found a singular voice and style.

Where, the Mile End is a collection of variousness: of disparate locations and intercut scenes. The scattered sequence of poems entitled 'Waterloo Sunset's Fine' grounds the collection amidst all of its travel, becoming a formal anchoring point to which the reader often returns. There are sprinkled allusions to politics and to poets, including TS Eliot ('by the end of April the city softens / knows it has been cruel', from 'Removal'), and Seamus Heaney: a figure central to Morrissy's perception of 'home', or lack thereof. '[N]obody is from where I'm from', begins 'Wake', and its sentiment is echoed at the beginning of 'Landscape': 'there is no turf where I'm from'. 'Wake' ends with the speaker returning, if only imaginatively, to Northern Ireland, with another nod to Heaney:

> meanwhile, my mind is flown
> by the men in sensible brown shoes
> gathered at the soft mud at Mossbawn

America and Ireland merge in 'The Last Resort' as 'the edges of Doonbeg' – home to the American president's hotel and golf course – 'are collapsing / slipping from the links / straight into the Atlantic'. Wry and cynical, Morrissy examines the resort's environmental consequences ('you'll be able to swim to the Aran Islands soon / or walk / on newly formed ocean spit'), and ends pointedly: 'some things are just for you'. In minimally punctuated free verse, Morrissy weaves the personal and the political, notes lists and landscapes, and crystallises insight into striking images – 'the leaves in the driveway press together / curling as inverted parachutes' ('Grounding').

As a reader who, admittedly, gravitates towards traditional forms and neatly boxed stanzas, a collection of free verse originally felt daunting. Yet witnessing the ways in which Morrissy's poems unfold on the page – unfold in time, are interrupted, return to where they were – it is clear they could not have been constructed in any other form. These poems are moments in time, and are experienced as such. Morrissy has a fine ear for assonance and internal rhyme, and an intuitive command of lineation, spacing, and alignment. Beneath these seemingly free-form, deceptively simple poems lies logical patterning and incredibly careful formatting.

As the lines traverse sweeping, shifting landscapes, there is comfort to be found in the stability and consistency of the lyric 'I' in *Where, the Mile End*. This singular voice guides the reader through the collection's ever-changing settings, and a sense of 'home' manifests in its quotidian moments. The reader accompanies Morrissy through such scenes: buying groceries, reading in un-Irish sun, cycling home 'half drunk half exhausted', and assembling Swedish flat-pack furniture. *Where, the Mile End* is a collection of sensory reflections and interconnected journeys, that often return – albeit changed – to where they began. They are narratives of exploration in which, as Morrissy acknowledges in 'Looped', 'everything leads back to Bull Island / and the North Strand'.

The poems in *Flèche*, the debut collection from Mary Jean Chan, remain more rooted. These poems are vessels for a set of looping thematic strands: daughterhood, language, culture, queerness, and love. With meticulous care, Chan's poems articulate intergenerational family dynamics; the word 'mother' is present in almost every poem, and 'love' occurs nearly as frequently. The title, *Flèche*, is a cross-linguistic pun. Pronounced 'flesh' (an implicit, third layer of meaning), the term is an offensive technique used in fencing, and also the French word for 'arrow'. Terms from fencing structure the collection, which is divided into three sections: 'Parry', 'Riposte', and 'Corps-À-Corps'. Within this structure, the poems are complicit in a series of 'moves' and 'turns' that demonstrate simultaneous violence and beauty.

Although these poems are thematically repetitive, this tunnel vision makes for an immersive reading experience, as the world of *Flèche* assembles itself through each poem. Previous dynamics are recast in a new light, while figures that populate the poems become more knowable: characters in their own poetic world. Although images are repeated, Chan is continually finding new forms for them, and the shapes her poems take are admirably dynamic. 'To the Grandmother Who Mistook Me for a Boy' wears its sonnet-status lightly, almost as an afterthought, as simple rhyming words step around one another elegantly before settling on its final couplet. In 'the five stages', Chan maps a narrative of love, and acceptance, onto the five stages of grief, using a double oblique, or forward slash, in substitution for line-breaks: 'I am sitting in my friend's room // her smile is in the shape of a question // *have you ever wondered if you might like women* // I stare back at her // willing composure'. This oblique is a multifaceted symbol, and in the poem entitled '/ /' these lines signify both chopsticks and lovers:

> My mother lays the table with chopsticks & ceramic
> spoons, expects you to fail at dinner. To the Chinese,
>
> you & I are chopsticks: lovers with the same anatomies.

'/ /' and 'The Window' have both been shortlisted for the Forward Prize for Best Single Poem (2017 and 2019, respectively), and 'The Window' was also awarded second prize in the 2017 National Poetry Competition. Ending with 'the slightest touch of grace', this poem exemplifies the calm assuredness that distinguishes Chan's poetic voice.

Salt is a recurring image in *Flèche*, symbolic of all that has been pre-served, and passed, between generations. In 'Flesh', the poet's mother seasons wounds, and salt becomes shorthand for past grievances. In 'That Child is My Mother', the mother remains haunted by her memories of the Great Chinese Famine, and 'would raid the fridge at midnight for a salted egg, some pickled carrots', while in a later poem ('They Would Have All That'), 'too much salt brings back / / the years of loneliness'. In the tender 'Rules for a Chinese Child Buying Stationery in a London Bookshop', generational wisdom is found in the untranslatable proverb *'having had more salt / than you have eaten rice'*, while the young boy is promised 'a lifetime ahead of you, / years of salt / and rice and tea'.

There are further attempts to convey the untranslatable. In '/ /', for example, 'expletives detonate' and are glossed in English: '[*two / / women*] [*two men*] [*disgrace*]'. 'I have never said *mother* / my entire life', proclaims the speaker of 'This Grammatical Offer of Uniqueness is Untrue', questioning the poet's decision to write through these experiences – and her mother's experiences – in English. The opening poem, 'My Mother's Fables', narrates personal history, demonstrating the power of storytelling to keep family history alive. Fable and fairytale run through this collection; writing of her fellow fencers in 'Practice', Chan observes 'I thought we were / / princes in a fairy tale with a twist, since / there were no princesses to be taken'.

Sincerity can sometimes feel like a lost art in poetry, though the concept colours all of Chan's work. Inevitably biographical, *Flèche* reads as a poetic *Bildungsroman*, articulating its way towards freedom and acceptance. With its characters 'hungry for food or love', *Flèche* is an accomplished collection – from an already accomplished poet – about ache and desire. Its poems provide wisdom for 'holding the heart's ache at bay', in a collection humming with love.

Last Spring, I was fortunate enough to catch Rachael Allen reading from her first collection, *Kingdomland*, at the Shakespeare and Company bookshop in Paris. Listening to Allen – with her intensely unique reading style – my partner, leaning over, added to my notes: *She is cool*. Amended, moments later, it read: *She is cool and weird*. This striking, fiery collection is 'cool' and 'weird' to the extreme. *Kingdomland* is a series of dark, surreal worlds that feel like dreamscapes, and is an impressive, fiercely original debut from the current poetry editor at Granta Publications.

The collection opens onto a world already in flames: 'Watch the forest burn / with granular heat.' Allen writes a world of archetypes, of violent men and vulnerable women, of animals and children, and there is a sense in these poems of ever-looming danger. *Kingdomland*, as Allen explains it, is inspired by Cornwall, where the poet was born. One can see how Cornwall, with its superstitious magic and rugged landscapes, has inspired the beauty and darkness of these poems. Allen's surreal narratives are evocative of fairytales, though not in the classical manner of Mary Jean Chan. Her poems are bizarre and surreal, bordering always upon nightmares.

Transformation is central to this collection, and 'Promenade' demonstrates how this may be achieved within just twelve lines. The poem's romantic landscape – 'I walk by the carriage of the sea' – is undercut by the assaulting 'vinegar wind'. This love poem is quickly derailed, becoming violent and strange, as its initial image – 'Openly wanting something / like the opened-up lungs of a singer' – is warped. 'I'll just lie down, / my ribs opened up in the old town square / and let the pigs root through my chest' is a dark transformation of its beginning, the desired 'opened-up lungs of a singer' made literal through the 'opened up' body, the speaker's open 'wanting' granted through a dark parallelism.

The titular 'Kingdomland' is Allen at her very best. Initially seeming to belong to the realm of fairytale, with the 'dark village' that 'sits on the crooked hill', the narrative quickly turns surreal:

>   I am walking towards a level crossing,
>   while someone I love is jogging into the darkness.
>   *Come away from there*, I am yelling,
>   while the black dog rolls in the twilit yard.
>   Small white socks bob into the dark like teeth in the mouth
>   of a laughing man, who walks backwards into night,
>   throwing drinks into the air
>   like a superstitious wife throws salt.

Rachael Allen is adept at creating strangeness, and unexpected shifts in tense, person, and place leave the reader frequently disarmed. Her images are assertively creative, with evening 'coming down like hair snipped over shoulders' (from the sequence 'Nights of Poor Sleep'), and 'simple' men described as 'Under-lit like a driveway' ('Simple Men').

Allen's voice is at its most confident in staccato declaratives, and her use of adverbs is particularly fine: 'the moon sways over me whitely', while 'trees darkly mask the sky' ('Nights of Poor Sleep'), and in *Rodeo fun on a Sunday*, 'the sun begins to thinly shine at dawn'. Further highlights (in a luminous collection) include 'Monstrous Horses', 'Volcano', and 'Prawns of Joe'. The first poem in *Kingdomland* speaks of a girl who 'floats up' against a burning landscape. In the final poem, this girl is pluralised, united in numbers. *Kingdomland* begins in charred dystopia and ends in ambiguity – part violent and part triumphant – 'as the girls float up / to the billowing ceiling'.

Eiléan Ní Chuilleanáin

IN THE COSMOS

Dorothy Molloy, *The Poems of Dorothy Molloy* (Faber and Faber, 2019), £16.99 hb.

The title poem of Dorothy Molloy's first collection, *Hare Soup* (2004), ends with an explosion of competing reds. There is (typically, if rather mildly, for her) the collision with the body, 'bouquets of old-fashioned roses / fall into my lap'. But the roses are:

> ... petals shot with bright flashes
> of scarlet and purple, vermilion, alizarin,
> ruby, carmine and cerise.

It's almost a summary of what makes her work special: a body's presence, the bold matching of hot colours, the slightly exotic, slightly technical vocabulary owing something to her years as a painter; and there's also the juxtaposition of this visual feast with the rank smell, evoked by the title and emphasised earlier in the poem, as it emanates from the 'foul-smelling kitchen'.

All those reds are there to describe the blood shed when the speaker fends off a sexual assault, with violent reprisal and apparent relish, in a poem full of voracious appetites. Blood, particularly the wild shock of *seeing* blood, reappears in 'Was it like this?' and 'First Blood', where men are again brutal, maddened by the thought of the female's experience, or just by her existence. Many of these poems get their energy from a simultaneous attraction and repulsion when faced with the reality of the alien, whether the other is merely masculine, or set apart by disease, or foreign – her many years in Spain supply numerous presences, though the opening poems of *Hare Soup* are set in France.

That first collection, as we know, was also almost posthumous, copies of the book arriving in the week of the poet's death. So it's her readers who have had to mature, or to learn her idiom, in a process that seems the reverse of the ordinary, as two further books, *Gethsemane Day* and *Long-distance Swimmer*, appeared in the five years after her death; this collected volume includes forty more poems that were never published. We might expect her to be progressively less present, as we move from the finished, printed, and approved collections, to posthumous books assembled by her husband Andrew Carpenter, to work from notes and corrected typescripts. However, any apprehended attrition is countered by her weighty assertion, also from a notebook, the one where she wrote her last poems. Its first sentence suggests the packed energy that is not dissipated by her death: 'The one essential thing is for my voice to ring out in the cosmos and to use, to this end, every available second.' The new book demands to be read in the light of this challenge to herself, to her resolve.

Some poems in *Hare Soup* had appeared in magazines before 2004. One I remember in particular, 'Cast Out', where the speaker has an unclean antagonist, definitely female, the two bound together – one feeding the other. It is an exciting poem for me, since I still recall the pleasure and surprise I felt when it landed in the post as a submission to *Cyphers*. Its imagery, pillaged from the Old Testament, is about the ceremonial uncleanness of leprosy; the setting of the poem on the other hand is medieval – correctly, as those taboos were alive and well in the European Middle Ages – but its climate seems to me to be timeless, it's about an instinctive bodily withdrawal from something that reeks of pollution:

> She circles my walled city with her clappers and her cup.
>
> From battlement and organ-loft I throw her food to eat:
> unleavened bread, goat's cheese, the flesh of swine.

The menu draws almost gleefully on the repertoire, piling up uncleannesses, and even worse, mixing the clean and unclean together. The greatest taboo being death, and worse still, the failure to die:

> I sprinkle her with clay, ignore her cries. I turn away
>
> to ring the Requiem bell. She joins the living dead.
> At Mass I see her lean into the leper-squint, receive
>
> from some gloved hand the Sacred Host.

'Cast Out' is strongly exotic with its church imagery and its leper-squint, but it expresses a sense of visceral horror that is not antiquarian. Dorothy Molloy had lived in places where the Middle Ages were close and their inheritance almost intact, and the labile shudder between the speakable and unspeakable comes from an awareness of continuity that is instinctive, not just in Spain but in Ireland too. It is not a vague sense of the past but is based on real knowledge of attitudes and codes. In 'Sipping vodka' (*Long-distance Swimmer*) the snowy Alps seen from a plane recall 'cathedrals / of ice. Flying buttresses / rise to meet me. Gargoyles / monkey about.' The eye has been trained to find the meanings in an ecclesiastical system.

The almost-synaesthesia of her poems owes much to her European, especially Spanish, experience; the assault of colour, smells, noise, heat, food deployed to shock her readers into allowing sensation and desire to get worryingly close. In the later poems too, Spain and her life there refuse to be pushed into the background. Throughout her work the country is evoked as the place where realities of passion, colour, loathing and sudden desire, people in extremity, are most fully present. Ireland is cooler, does not set out to make itself interesting; it is the enabling scene for poems about houses, animals, families, and some terrifying pieces about hospitals. In 'Grandma's Zoo' (*Hare Soup*), the zoo is populated by the animals on the old Irish coinage, but the coin that is given as 'a charm against the elephant-man / who comes bellowing to my bed' is doubtfully effective.

Dorothy Molloy had access to some mental space where wild ideas we might want to dismiss to the past are alive and forceful. Frightening pressures are conjured and moulded; when 'Cast Out' ends with 'I wear beneath my robe her running sores', the present tense is not chosen lightly. The body in her poems lives in the present; it leans towards the non-human world. In 'Envelope of Skin' (*Hare Soup*), we view 'The caterpillar of my / spine. The wide plates / of my hips.' She hovers on the borders of shock much of the time, but her speech is generally far from plain, it is a modern bardic idiom, full of words *recherchés* in both the English and French senses, with a crammed syntax and sharply edged lines, particularly in *Hare Soup*. *Gethsemane Day* and *Long-distance Swimmer* contain poems as striking as that first collection, with others that seem more relaxed and less packed.

The unpublished poems – what about them? The reader may miss the reassurance of a poet's *imprimatur*. Looking at an accomplished poem – and there are many fine ones: 'Nutrient pollution in Lake Chapala', 'Mother', 'In Guadalupe', 'Memory jolts' are just a few – we might wonder whether it might have ended up being recast as something else, or whether it might be evidence of a new direction. But this is a consequence of the way poetry has been packaged in our day. The first readers of 'Pangur Bán' did not ask such questions.

Among the late pieces are longish poems which might indeed be part of a new turn: one on the life of Catherine the Great, one, 'I gave away my luck', a tale of a love triangle. 'The seer of Tremvan' is about John Gwenogvryn Evans, the Welsh scholar who was obsessed with Taliesin: a whole life in a poem. Another, perhaps from an earlier period, about the resort village of Alcossebre – between Barcelona and Valencia – is an exploration of a place. These all suggest that the narrative spine of so many of the published poems might have been developed into a fully ribbed and feathered narrative poetry. Dorothy Molloy, we know, frequented a writing group, and that may account for the presence of (for my taste) far too many villanelles. Curse of the poetry workshop and the creative writing course, they display her control of form – but her poems in whatever shape are always well formed, usually in ways that do not distract the reader from what is being communicated. I was cheered by 'Villanelle of the Bilbao babies' which sends up the form with high-spirited rhymes on 'jangles', 'wrangles', 'bangles', and 'dangles'. The concluding quatrain opens with 'My heart is squashed by twenty-seven mangles', which reminds me to point out that her poems, in a number of ways, are great fun to read.

Liam Carson

CYBORGS, COLONIALISM, AND THE GHOST IN THE MACHINE

Sally Wen Mao, *Oculus* (Graywolf Press, 2019), $16.
Franny Choi, *Soft Science* (Alice James Books, 2019), $15.95.

> ... Darlings, let's rewrite
> the script. Let's hijack the narrative, steer
>
> the story ourselves.
> – 'ANNA MAY WONG STARS AS CYBORG #86'

The title of Sally Wen Mao's second collection, *Oculus*, is a key to its concerns. From the Latin, it can mean a circular opening in a dome or in a wall; it acts both as a drain and as a source of light; it is cleansing and illuminating. Sight, both in real and virtual worlds, is central. In her first poem, she sets out her terms:

> Forgive me if the wind stole
> the howl from my mouth and whipped
> it against your windowpanes.
> When I lived, I wanted to be seen.

'Ghost Story' is replete with images of vision experienced in myriad ways – in a 'mansion made of windows'; on a 'plasma television'; where wolves are caught in searchlights; objects are seen through binoculars.

Speech and silence are core to the narrative structure of much of *Oculus*. The poems unfurl stories within stories. Hence, we have marvellous poems about Anna May Wong, a 1920s silent film star, who inhabits a world of silence:

> It is natural to live in an era
>   when no one uttered –
> and silence was glamour
>   – 'ANNA MAY WONG ON SILENT FILMS'

Wong is seen through Western eyes, cast through the prism of Orientalist tropes: 'White men gazed down my neck like wolves' ('Anna May Wong Blows Out Sixteen Candles'). She is a femme fatale with murder in her gaze: 'If they didn't murder / me, I died of an opium overdose'. 'The Toll of the Sea' includes italicised lines from the film of the same title, a retelling of *Madame Butterfly*. Wong tells how she is *'Alone in a stranger's garden'*. She takes a time machine to the future, where she thinks she will be cast as 'some girl from L.A., the unlikely heroine', rather than 'another / Mongol slave' ('Anna May Wong Fans Her Time Machine'). Wong herself travels to a new life in America, lured by *'the siren sea, whose favors are a mortgage upon the soul'* ('The Toll of the Sea'). The concubine protagonist of 'Mutant Odalisque' is, like Wong, seen as an object, a woman trapped in the 'craven lens' of a webcam, trying to make her 'witnesses' see her as 'No machine'.

Mao rewrites Wong's history, and the history of relations between the West and China. 'Let's hijack the narrative, steer // the story ourselves', she declares ('Anna May Wong Stars as Cyborg #86'). *Oculus* is an Asian Futurist text, saturated with technological and science fiction imagery, but it also looks back to a history of colonialism, one defined by invasion and conquest:

> An East India Company, an opium trade,
> a war, a treaty, a concession, an occupation

Mao is aware that 'recovering the silenced history' is not 'as simple as smashing its container' ('Occidentalism'). The colonial mindset lives on in the 'tome of hegemony'. The power of the Western gaze, its urge to possess what it sees, is everywhere. Capitalist ownership of the body itself is taken to an extreme in 'Provenance: A Vivisection', which draws on a controversy surrounding the Bodies World Exhibition, in which it was alleged that plastinated bodies on display belonged to Chinese dissidents. The exhibition is 'a factory / of muscle', 'an empire / of polymer'. Humans are reduced to meat, 'hanging organs' in 'an abattoir of gratitude'.

'We're not in Polanski's / Chinatown anymore', Mao pointedly comments in 'Anna May Wong Stars as Cyborg #86', smartly referencing *The Wizard of Oz*. She reveals early Chinese-American history in the extended ballad 'The Diary of Afong Moy', a first-person narrative from the point of view of the first Chinese woman to come to the USA in 1834. Spectators paid to see her in exhibitions aimed at selling Chinese products to American whites, or in PT Barnum's carnival freak shows. She visits the Oval Office, where she sings with 'My whole / life in my throat', but finds 'my voice sounded ghastly', her words 'inscrutable' to her audience:

> The lyrics, if I remember –
> how a face conceals its intentions
> like a woman conceals her name.

Afong Moy travels to the antebellum South of Charleston, but dreams of home, 'the fishing village, the locust / tree near the river where I used to sit / with friends'. She weaves the reality of her father 'counting coins, scraping rice in his bowl' with the spectres in the South's cities and in the smell of 'the murders / in their field' (an echo of the 'scent of magnolias' in Billie Holiday's 'Strange Fruit'). Here are different American stories blending or reflecting each other, stories of slavery and subjugation.

If China is the 'old country', Mao also presents modern China as a potent new world. There's a ghostly gorgeousness to 'Close Encounters of the Liminal Kind' that reminds one of Marina Tsvetaeva's evocations of an icy Moscow. She traverses China's vast distances by train to her home city of Wuhan, with 'heat at the center of it'. 'Riding Alone for Thousands of Miles' has a Whitmanesque pulse in its incantatory litany of people and place, its definition of nation. It riffs beautifully on Woody Guthrie's 'This Land is Your Land' (and, again, *The Wizard of Oz*):

> This land promises snowfall. This land promises windfall.
> This land promises the return of brief days. May this land
> promise you a body, some muscle, some organ, a brain.

Mao's protagonist in 'Ghost in the Shell' – a poem about the manner in which white actress Scarlett Johansson was cast as a Japanese character – asks: 'do I dare proclaim, / with a cyborg body, this humanity is my own?'

Franny Choi also hones in on ghosts in the machine, and the poems of *Soft Science* are framed within the device of the Turing Test, a series of questions designed to detect for consciousness. Thus, a cyborg undergoes tests to determine empathetic response, boundaries, problem solving, and love. *Soft Science* is, in essence, a novel in verse seen through 'a flickering screen' or through the growing consciousness of a cyborg as she experiences hardness and softness – both emotional and physical – in human society. Thus, the cyborg enters into 'a soft wall / to drink the shock of touch' ('Perchance to Dream'), or says 'i have only ever wanted to bite down hard' ('& O Bright Star of Disaster, I Have Been Lit'). In 'Chi', we meet the broken android Chi from the manga *Chobits*, who is only too human in her physical anxieties, and in her unease with the consciousness she inhabits: '*in need of a shower ... unsure of my name; unformatted*'.

Trump's divided America of walls, border guards, and rampant racism is surely at the heart of 'You're So Paranoid' (a play on Carly Simon's 'You're So Vain'), where a 'wall of cops bucks like a frightened boar', becoming 'a wall of men standing on my friends' necks', while the cops move with 'a wall inside them'. In another poem, the cyborg watches a video of Nazis incapable of saying her name properly: 'o too / hard : for his kind : to pronounce' ('The Cyborg Watches a Video of a Nazi ...').

With each Turing Test, Choi's cyborg increasingly reveals her humanity, complete with memories of a native country: 'my body, my organic /

origin ... land my mother' ('Turing Test_Problem Solving'). The cyborg contemplates the language in which she expresses herself: 'there are many programming languages / use whichever you prefer ... it is yours / to make sing' ('Turing Test_Love'). There is the language the coloniser forces on the colonised: 'someone laughs and plants / his nipple on my tongue like a flag' ('Acknowledgements'). Then there is the abusive language of the modern internet troll. 'The Cyborg Wants to Make Sure She Heard You Right' is composed of offensive tweets directed at Choi herself – where she is insulted as an 'uppity, filthy immigrant girl' told to go back to a 'mudhole'. Choi takes this poisonous language, renders it into multiple languages through Google Translate, then translates it back into English, turning it back on its faceless authors:

> Each male is not shown. Only white hetero.
>   This is nothing. Cultural differences
> was a mistake. How crazy can not find her. Will be very pleased.
>   lol parody, written, or oil, to rage.

Choi reaches a lyrical peak in 'Perihelion: A History of Touch'. This is where the cyborg becomes most human, most alive, expressing herself through a series of sensual prose poems, each one named after a full moon – wolf, snow, worm, sturgeon, and so on. These shapeshifting poems speak from the mouths of flowers, fruit, fish, the cyborg's mind melding with nature itself: 'I picked up my own scent somewhere on the forest's edge. Spoiling flour, holy basil, sweat' ('Hunter's Moon'). The cyborg arrives fully at humanity by arriving at poetry.

In one Turing Test poem ('Turing Test_Weight'), we are told 'the question here is one of history, of a family tree'. *Soft Science* is nothing if not ambitious in its structure and in its concerns – technology, gender, politics, racism, biology, body image, and the nature of individual awareness. It's a book that needs to be read as one weave, and read in order, from start to finish.

Both Franny Choi and Sally Wen Mao see history through the lens of the future, through brilliantly imaginative science fiction strategies – creating poetry that is morally urgent, and utterly of our times.

Stiofán Ó Cadhla

THE CIVILISED ATLANTIC WAY

Paddy Bushe, *Móinéar an Chroí* (Coiscéim, 2018), €7.50.
Máire Dinny Wren, *Tine Ghealáin* (Éabhlóid, 2019), €14 hb.

At least part of the reason that poetry gives so much unprescribed pleasure is the licence it has to simply take or leave many of the drop-down or pop-up suggestions of imagined or synthetic realities. In this sense, this is a pair of pleasurable collections of poetry in the Irish language from opposite ends of the country, counties Kerry and Donegal, but with similar perspectives. Bushe and Wren are a pair, coupled by the intimate and interesting connections they make between memory, music, place, and people, in terms of the latter affirming some of the insights of North American anthropologist Keith H Basso (*Wisdom Sits in Places: Landscape and Language Among the Western Apache*, 1996).

Móinéar an Chroí is Paddy Bushe's third collection in Irish and is subdivided into sections comprised of original poems and translations. It opens with 'Móinéar', aesthetically measured, proportionate and tempered, evincing the craftiness of the poet's alignment of memory, music, and time. Although rhymes or regularities are rare, form and evenness is evident, especially early on. The first two verses of 'Púcaí' are deceptively poised, as words and music contest for primacy, untethering meaning from the word. With the 'camera obscura of the artist', he unveils invisible or nonverbal aspects of communication and reveals some of the discreet webs that link emotion to materiality.

The physical environment is alive in the toponymy of his beloved Iveragh peninsula, lending vivid lyricality and pictoriality to the poetry: there is scarcely a poem that isn't so placed or named. Nor is he afraid to defend it when he perceives a threat, in 'Reic na Sceilge', and here rhyme lends authority to condemnation as he objects to the State's shameless huckstering of heritage:

> Sceilg Mhichíl ar reic is ar díol
> Trí chamastaíl ghiollaí an stáit seo,
> A chúlaigh go rúnda ó chúram an dúchais
> Ar son scillingí suaracha *Star Wars*.

In 'Tech Amergin', corporate governance is faulted for subverting the community potential of the cultural centre of the same name:

> Béasa na mbroc bheith ag tochailt leo
> I bpluais a gcuid *corporate governance*;

> Cé gur pobal is bonn leis an ionad
> Spraoi ná scléip ann don bpobal ní toil leo.

Local temporal and cultural depth is a catalyst for a universal reversion, shared by both poets, which Bushe describes as 'claochló oirthearach Uíbh Ráthaigh' ('Sínithe'), instating an Iveragh orientality. A rapprochement is reached between the native local and the native universal, the re-articulated 'Forógra Aimhirghin' sits happily alongside the haiku. In fittingly dignified, heartfelt eulogies for two seafaring seers ('Kirby agus na Ba' for Mícheál Ua Ciarmhaic, 'An Eachtra Nua' for Domhnall Mac Síthigh), he imagines Ua Ciarmhaic as the fisherman on the great road beyond the Skellig Island, 'thar chaladh, / Is thar Sceilg Mhichíl amach', where the Gaeltacht of his soul circumscribes the whole realm. And he imagines Dónal Mac an tSíthigh, tragically drowned at sea, reaching the brightlands of story, 'gealchríoch na heachtraíochta', and telling a tale lasting the round of the year counted out by the ancient ancestral calendric measure from *Samhain* to *Bealtaine*.

The poet's quality is entirely encapsulated by 'Fardoras, Sceilg Mhichíl', the backbone of this collection, about a concealed cross on the underbelly of the lintel in an oratory on Skellig Michael. It is a testament to the poem's consistency and composure that it is a challenge to translate: the metronomic dripping of water, 'Chomh rialta céanna le cloigín éatrom'; the carpet silence of moss, 'I gciúnas an chaonaigh'; and a rivulet of light, 'Sníonn an solas'. The cross, once a headstone, is used by the monks to 'roof their prayers' and to 'spear any snake that might sneak beneath the threshold of their mind'. This is a beautiful poem worthy of the famed island and its devotees, an example of the splendid balance between perception, control, and craft in his best poems.

Moving down – or is it up? – north, *Tine Ghealáin* is Máire Dinny Wren's second collection, and it is a handsome and handy production, generous, fruitful and, not unlike the west Donegal landscape of *mín* and *creag*, both sharp and gentle. From the bleak prospect of 'Ar an Chladach Dhearóil' on the pollution of the sea, to the essay-like 'Bánú na Tuaithe', in which the dying embers give cold comfort and company as the wind knocks at the storm door, or 'doras na síne', here is a poet who allows words to breathe and resonate. The poet allows words their natural level in the avidly human and articulate Connellesque dialect ('tointeáil', 'ailleog', 'cróigeáin mhóna', 'bachtaí', 'canach', 'an chuach', 'sleamhnacháin', 'cróigeadh', 'stucaí', 'bladhaire'). It is deceptively casual, arising from a keen consciousness that is at home in the storied locale, mining and minting a rich quarry of memory. A personal and vernacular design or logic leads her bravely here and there, minding other ways and days from the insistent entropy of the present – in 'Fallaing an Fhómhair', the 'séideán sí' of memory wraps around her like her grandmother's cloak. Here, as she says in 'An Bocsadóir', every field and fence has a story. At times she perfects a lovely light touch with troubling subject matter, relying on the dialect's own age-honed precision, directness, and earthiness. It is a distinctively modern and native voice that can conjure beauty or poignancy even in a dark, apparently unnatural, dead end, as in 'Ag Gabháil 'na Bhaile':

> Tá na héanacha fiáine i bpatrún na gcuirtíní
> de shíor ag eitilt os do chionn,
> iad gafa go deo anseo i do sheomra
> is níl éalú i ndán dóibh ná duit.

Wren doesn't shy away from the atomisation felt in rural areas. In 'Ar an Iargúltacht', a woman sends letters to herself to bring someone to the door. Hope shines through like the white bog cotton on the black bog or the volubility of dancing swallows outside a window in 'Damhsa na bhFáinleog'. In 'Adharc Thoraí', when fog has consumed every landmark, the trombonic boom of the Tory foghorn heralds humanity's presence.

She instinctively inclines towards the natural and sensuous, and the collection assembles music, mermaids, trains, place-names, landscape and seascape, fiddles, melodeons, singers, turf cutters, bog cotton, and Colm Cille together. In 'Abhainn Chró na hUla' she avers that the music of the river, accompanied by the mazurkas and waltzes of her father's melodeon, is the soundtrack to her life. The very strain of sound or music, 'cuach' or 'cuaichín', ignites memories in 'Tine Ghealáin' and 'Ag Ceol go Fóill'. Anything that emits sound – lambs, rivers, church bells, wind or birds – is music, like the blackbird, again echoing early Irish lyrics, in 'Fonn an Loin Dhuibh', raising the heart; or in 'An Fidléir', where the birds attend in respect, and the music finally diffuses again from whence it came. The universal reversion is encapsulated in the nameless gems of haiku, crisp and clear, inserted throughout like free gifts. In 'Ag an Tobar Beannaithe' the pilgrim has sacred wisdom, 'eagnaíocht dhiaga', bestowed on him or her, and sings a song in propitiation. In 'Cantaireacht na Murúch', the roiling sea threatens to mute the songful mermaids rolling in the tide. Several poems intimate the silencing of the effulgent voice of hope that, in 'Gafa' and 'Pluais', subsists moth-like on even the slightest sliver of light. In the final poem, 'Mo Bhealach Féin', Wren thankfully renews her poetic vow, reasserting the integrity of the word, with a homage to local littérateur Seosamh Mac Grianna:

> Teannann téada mo ghutha le focail mo mheanman
> is le bé na héigse 'mo threorú téim mo bhealach féin.

And she continues on her own way and in good company.

Louise Leonard
$i^2 = j^2 = k^2 = ijk = -1$ (2019)
Etching, 36 x 48 cm

Louise Leonard
Still waters run deep (2019)
Etching, 36 x 48 cm

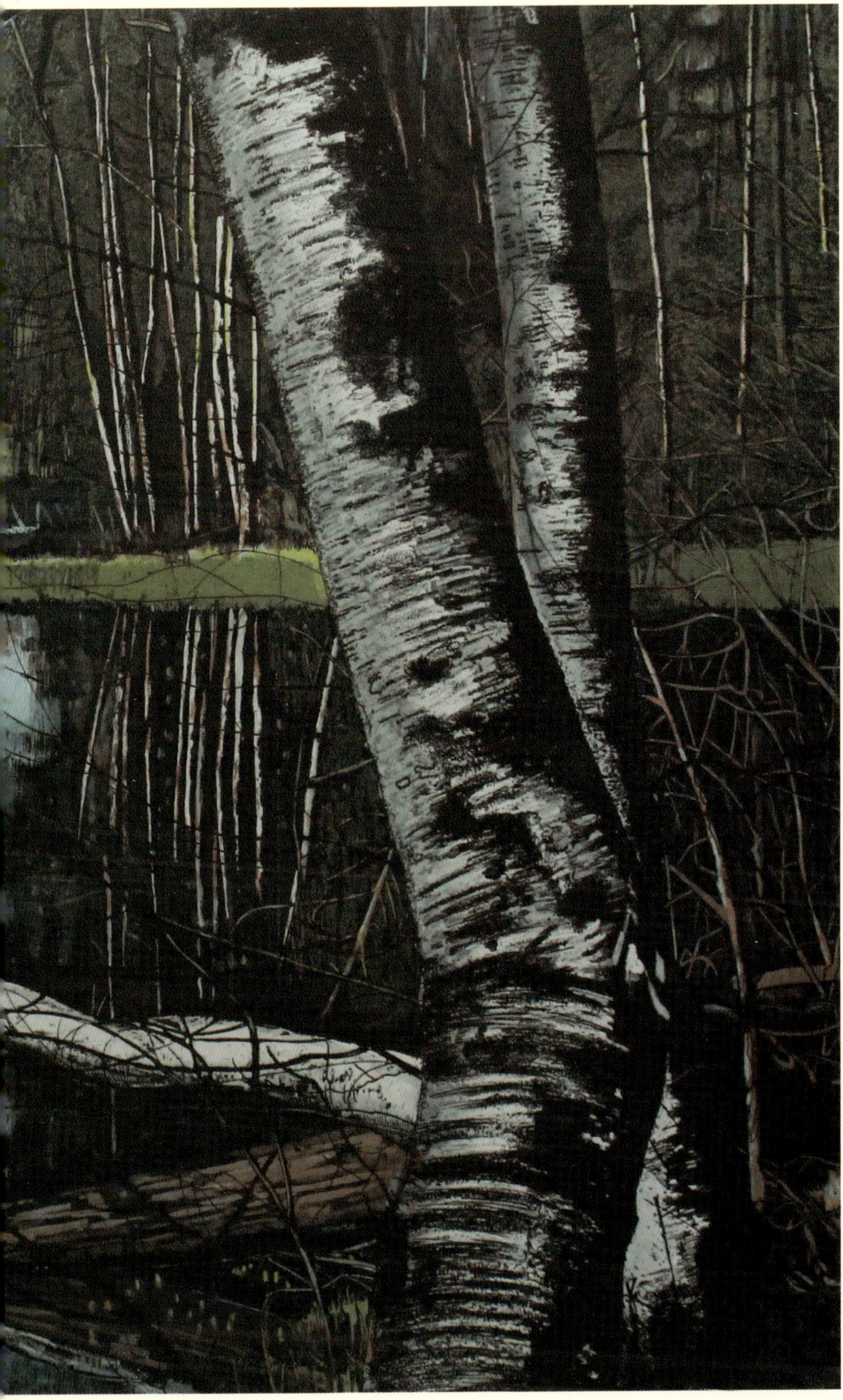

Louise Leonard
The green quiet (2019)
Etching, 36 x 28 cm

Louise Leonard
A heron goes hunting for sticklebacks (2019)
Etching, 48 x 36 cm

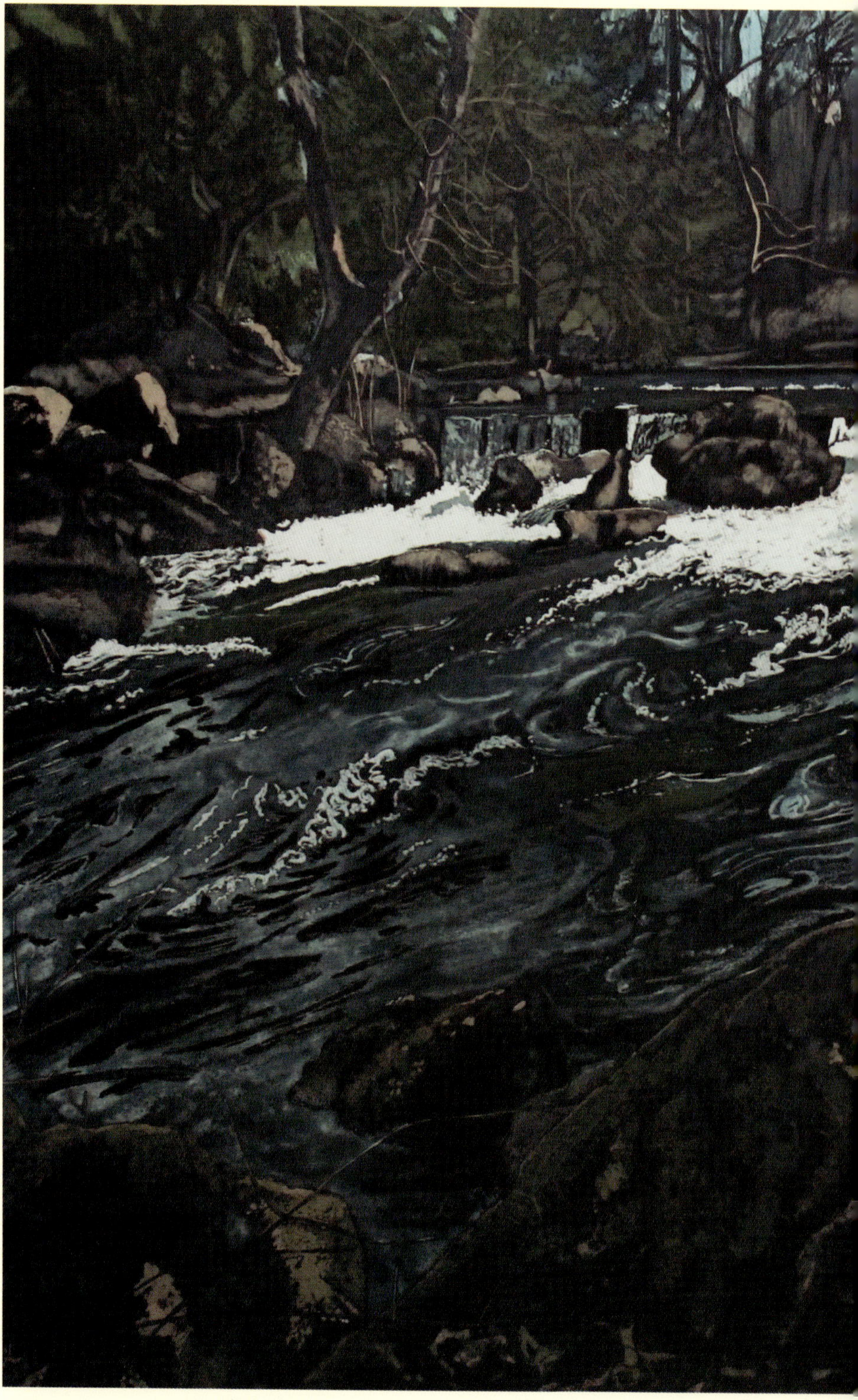

Louise Leonard
A river runs through it
Etching, 36 x 48 cm

Louise Leonard
Our lives like shadows come and go (2019)
Etching, 36 x 48 cm

https://graphicstudiodublin.com/artist/leonard-louise/

David Toms

FEEDING THE ENGINES

Christodoulos Makris, *this is no longer entertainment* (Dostoyevsky Wannabe, 2019), £8.
Matt Kirkham, *Thirty-Seven Theorems of Incompleteness* (Templar Poetry, 2019), £10 / €13.
Natasha Cuddington, *Each of us (our chronic alphabets)* (Arlen House, 2019), €13.

With so much of our public discourse now played out over the internet, that vast network of musings and meanderings has long been ripe as a source of found material for poets to work with. However, as we have lived longer with the internet and the internet as a thing has morphed, so too has our relationship with and to it. In her recent ground-breaking work, *The Age of Surveillance Capitalism*, Shoshana Zuboff has finally managed to put a name to what the internet is being purposed for: our 'behavioural surplus'. Rather than the asinine assertion that if the product is free you are the product, Zuboff's work convincingly charts instead the contention that, in fact, it is our behaviour that is the product – the behaviour we initially feed to the search engines, social media networks, and news sites, and eventually the behaviour that the internet tries to predetermine and direct us towards.

It is one part of the raw material of our behavioural surplus which Christodoulos Makris repurposes in the poems that make up *this is no longer entertainment*. That title is itself a stark warning, as strong as Zuboff's core argument in *The Age of Surveillance Capitalism*. Makris uses comments and other user-generated material from websites – the behavioural surplus which many of us are guilty of giving freely – to create a sustained and at times terrifying glimpse of the world as it now exists. What began as the diversionary act of commenting below the line, whiling away idle time online, has become an all-consuming part of the public discourse. It has shaped it, transformed it, created a kind of monster – a host of monsters indeed. We talk less to one another because we type more. We comment, and we get stuck into preposterous arguments that go nowhere. Reading *this is no longer entertainment*, in which lots of online commentary is stripped of its original context, one still feels the enduring sense of vertigo that can easily be achieved by going 'below the line' on almost any news article, video, or other piece of online content:

> Unless it's toilet graffiti or schoolyard banter at a
> family wedding it goes right over my head which

> is why (takes a deep breath and holds head defiantly
> high) I don't understand poetry at all. Nobody calls
> Leonard Cohen a pervert.

Like the internet it draws inspiration from, the poems in this book offer a heady mix of gratuitous sexual imagery, violence, and much of the other ugly reality that people feel freer in expressing online than they (might) feel comfortable expressing in the 'real world':

> Many days I walked in the rain rather
> than get a non-Irish taxi. Starving Ethiopians in the
> 1980's was it? Live Aid to feed them? Well look at
> the big strong Africans in Dundalk now, well able
> to drive a taxi and claim dole at the same time.

And of course, this too is part of the point and the problem. We talk about the online and offline, although the line between one and the other – as Zuboff's work demonstrates – is thin to vanishing now. Makris's poems reinforce this. The incongruous encounters of the online comment section, where people hide behind handles and other forms of anonymisation, have in the years since his project began spilled out into the offline world. It may no longer be entertainment, but it has become decidedly more vital to engage with: our world is being shaped by the online discourses which these poems upend. In that way, to read these poems is to see the decontextualized nightmarish qualities of them in a way that indicates that we may have to work harder to fight against their worst excesses and outcomes. Makris has taken our behavioural surplus and fed it back to us as art, and it is terrifying.

Though it leaves less to chance and algorithms, nevertheless Matt Kirkham's *Thirty-Seven Theorems of Incompleteness* uses the logic of mathematics to tell through poetry the story of logician Kurt Gödel and his wife Adele, as they move from the disappearing world of the Habsburg empire, in which Gödel was born, to Princeton in post-war America. Gödel is chiefly remembered among mathematicians and logicians for his Incompleteness theorem. This reviewer can state with complete honesty that the implications of this are entirely beyond his ken. The extent to which mathematics impacts the poetry Kirkham writes is nonetheless worth considering. There is clear use of mathematical phraseology across the poems, and these fortunately do not prohibit one from enjoying the poems on their own terms, in the main. Across Kirkham's thirty-seven poems there are a set of poems linked 'Successor of Zero', followed by 'Successor of Successor of Zero' and so on, out to 'Successor of Successor of Successor of Successor of Successor of Zero'. Each of these poems shares a similar structure – a large block of prose text followed by three short lines. These five poems form a kind of thread across the wider collection, detailing the couple's life in Princeton and mixing it with memories of Gödel's boyhood in Brünn (Brno in the Czech Republic).

Two poems, however, stand out above all others in the collection: 'Notes on Number Theory for Those Who Would Travel to Europe', and 'After Lotte Reiniger'. Reiniger these days is remembered for her film *The Adventures of Prince Achmed* (1926), a stop-motion animation using paper cut-out techniques. It is the oldest surviving animated feature film, and was filmed frame-by-frame at 24 frames per second. Similarly, the poem builds in a sequence, moving from one line to two to four to eight and then sixteen, before degrading in a similar fashion from the peak to eight to four to two to one. The viewing of the film is a transportation device for Kurt and Adele 'that is the distance from here that we will always carry with us / whenever we finally go, after they are reunited / time and again, and in the cinema, thinking of middle Europe'. This is the crux of the entire collection – the melancholy felt by many of Gödel's generation for the lost world of the Austro-Hungarian Empire, the sundering of their world by two world wars. Despite being born in what is now the Czech Republic, Gödel considered himself Austrian first and foremost. It is perhaps telling that the book opens with a quote from another putatively Czech author, Franz Kafka: 'Logic is doubtless unshakable, but it cannot withstand a man who wants to go on living.' Gödel's example of living on and living with his love Adele, in a new world thoroughly removed from that in which they grew up, is at the core of Kirkham's collection, and is the spur that keeps the book from collapsing under the weight of the mathematical elements.

Natasha Cuddington's *Each of us (our chronic alphabets)* is as expansive and engaging a selection of poems as those to be found in either of the two other books, and as formally inventive as anything you are likely to read this year from an Irish poetry publisher. The three poems that make up this collection, and the accompanying notes which extend the conceit of all three, might have at one time seemed like a bolt from the blue for a female poet in the Irish context. Instead, Cuddington's work fits neatly within an expanding tradition of formally inventive poetry, ranging from the work of Catherine Walsh (*City West*), Anamaría Crowe-Serrano (*Crunch*), and recent work from Kimberly Campanello (*MotherBabyHome*) and Christine Murray (*bind*). What might once, in the parlance of our age, have seemed 'disruptive' or 'innovative', is less shocking to well-trained eyes. It is no longer the case that Irish poetry – that vast and varied entity – cannot accommodate such poetry as part of its own tradition.

The three poems – '*from* Parhelia', '*from* Grace', and 'Print' – are a tour-de-force. There is a sparseness that invites rapid reading, the emptiness of the pages providing room for the few words left to really breathe. The haptic quality of the mark-making and the typesetting bring us into a world that is future and past all at once. This is alluded to by the cover, two images of 'sundogs' or parhelia, from past centuries. Cuddington teases a little in 'Print' when she writes –

> unlike this poem, For Which there is beginning&
> no end,
> [...]
> Print is proofed And
> set again quoins tightened loosed w / their key
>
> But Once pigment, its soiled finger kiss
> that page
>
>   into the Hereafter ...

– and also reminds us of 'Newly muscled arm Which knows / How letters use their words'.

    Words and meanings, the rules of language, are stretched to the point of collapse in these poems. Comprehension is not only to be found in word order, but in disorder: eschewing the conventional opens up meaning and the potential of meaning. The effect is a powerful one, rare and captivating, like the parhelia that are a core influence.

Ruth McIlroy

TO TRICKY MARGARET, WHO HAD SPREAD
A SLANDEROUS ACCOUNT OF THE POETESS

No, Margaret, you trickster, why did you spread one wrong story
that a babe who was not baptised was in my womb;
why not pronounce the truth as surely as I do?
Not alike my father, you slanderer, and yours.
Not equal were my brothers and your unlovely louts.
Not alike were our homes.
Bones of wild venison were found in my father's house;
in your father's house were bree, and fish bones your fare.
As I climb from the town, my step is heavy and reserved.
I am ill-pleased with the hussy who hatched that lie story,
the basest refuse of the folk, a light jade without cattle.

Acknowledgement: 'A Satirical Song' from The Matheson Collection; *Gaelic songs of Mary MacLeod*

Alan Gillis

SCAFFOLDING

I set to work, try to compose myself
but all is construction, the whang and scuff

of a worksite out my window: the pile driver's graunch,
the bulldozer's crunch, the concrete mixer's motor-grind;

and my mind collapses to a clunch of greybricked
rubble-mess, gravel-dust; the grey-gunged leaks

of mortar streams, hose streaks; while pork-bellied men
in high-viz *hey!* hardhats *ho!* clang in commotion

so if I open my window for air
I meet the fair smiling crack of a builder's arse

then settle back in my orthopaedic deskchair
to demolish, build, demolish, build, demolish, build this verse.

Alan Gillis

DIONYSUS IN BELFAST

Big Andy, Wee Eddie, Fat Bobby and Sandy
in a BMW teeming with Lynx,
Blue Stratos, Brut, Old Spice,
catch sight of a foreign-looking glipe

on the pavement. "I look for The Limelight,"
he says, and Eddie says "Boys I thinks
we got one," the fluffy dice
above the dashboard chuckling yok-yok-yok.

So they drag him in and race
for the estate, all bonhomie and shit-talk
but Sandy's thinking twice:
something about that strange-eyed face.

"This is not The Limelight,"
says yer fella, and when Sandy says "look
we can double-back, let him be,"
Wee Eddie's yelling the odds: "Ye spooked-

out-pinko-Barbarella-yella poof!"
Then the stranger sets free
his own weird hoo-hoo-hoo
and it's like his hair has dyed itself bright

green and is shooting up like a tree
through the roof of the Beemer
floating through the night's sea
of wine, fluffy dice bulging like grapes

and Big Andy, queasier than on bonfire
night feels a tongue lick his skin,
tendrils bind his limbs, while Wee Eddie's
nose grows, and grows, to a moon-white

two-foot beak and Fat Bobby reeks
of kippers and lets out a backseat squawk
like Flipper. All turned dolphin, piss-streaks
through the night, they scoot off, diving for Belfast Lough.

Gerard Smyth

THE RAIN IN ARMAGH

Where and when we crossed the border
was something we never noticed.
No one announced it.
We saw no line in the road,
felt no change in the atmosphere

or sudden acceleration of heartbeat
as we crossed over.
The rain that rippled the Boyne
was the same as the rain in Armagh.
Above us no break in the clouds.

The green of the North
looked like the green of the South.
No shade of difference between them.
Slieve Gullion was as mystical
as the Cooley Peninsula,

the route of the *Táin*. So if a border exists
let the border guards remain invisible,
let the traveller come and go
like the sparrows who never stop to think
Where are we now ...

Gerard Smyth

AMERICAN POETS

1.

Impeccably dressed for dinner at seven;
hands washed clean to wipe away all medical smells,
the intense fragrance of *Queen Anne's Lace*.
It was all a trick of imagination –
the life he lived in Rutherford, New Jersey –
seeing things that astonished him *beyond words*:
all local wonders, the trivia poets spurned,
his years of cutting the cord between mother and child.
Knowing each face for miles around,
hearing the town breathe in, breathe out, he wished
he could give the pure air in that picture of Breughel's
hunters to workers with smoke in their lungs.
A midnight walk, a visit to *Paterson Falls* –
the water falling in symmetries.
Or a Saturday movie in Cinemascope after browsing
the downtown bookstores in search of Chinese poets.

2.

The people in his poems had no winter clothes –
the convicts and cripples,
the fugitive down to his bones.
His images were spare: those Indian ponies
coming out of the willows, the buffalo-killers
he saw in his dreams, twilights on the Mississippi.
He could always find words to describe
late afternoon in the fields of Ohio,
the loneliness of the Midwest; or how autumn
changes the appearance of streets in a factory town.

He heard a new language in bread lines and freight yards –
a prayer no longer in the noose of iambics
but in the rattle of empty beer cans,
a stadium cheer for the quarterback.
He could always find words to describe
the craftsman of hammers and wood
and the man with all the bad luck
stumbling into American weather, waving his list of regrets.

Afric McGlinchey

HELICO

Like a sunflower following light,
I am transfixed by the patterns:
these marble mosaics,
avenues of trees hung with oranges,
palms tall as a spire, Jacob's Ladder,
frothed at the top.
The waves lash on and on,
as though change is unthinkable.
That mythic, earlier flood
poured over all error,
wiping clean the new land with its salt.
This Holocene, where teens
scream into mikes, and icebergs
and reefs predict our extinction,
seems irreversible.
Can there be any remedy
other than nature's
mayhem democracy?
The earth has never felt more wondrous
than now, on this brink,
ladder and oranges teetering.

Rebecca Morgan Frank

LIONFISH ROBOT

Its beauty may paralyze you
        there in the deep,
all spine and line and hunger,

hoovering up the eggs, the little
        fish, lobster, grouper,
snapper – the list keeps growing of those

shrinking at the mouth of this sexed-up
        invader mating
and feeding the reefs into oblivion.

So we'll rip out those vicious little spears
        and adorn ourselves,
suck it up with our giant robot lips, try

to destroy the flamboyant manes we
        brought here
to the wrong ocean to begin with.

We will build a silicon doppelgänger
        of this little destroyer,
make it blood vessels to fill.

Fuel it with something like our blood,
        fuel it to travel farther,
last longer. This is a first step.

Liz Quirke

GOING TO GROUND

    hope he's holed up in an archive of weekend melodies
memories of how after breakfast they would dance
   been advised to dig, keep sinking a spade till I hit hell
or acceptance, but this is beyond me, a mirage of the fires that stole
    my sleep when lullabies were my parents' low voices
lilting up through the floorboards. My dreams now see him dead
    and he offers his armchair to soothe my rattling bones
he knows I've never spoken about being alone in the house
    after leaving the hospital for the first time. I used my old key
slipped through, spectral behind his cars, fired up the Land Rover
    and frightened poor Brigitta across the road
How I didn't know we would rely on the aul stock
    Sonya and her mother and their bags of tea and biscuits
the way I was quick to introduce my wife, even though
    it has been decades since we spent evenings playing kerbs
They're all gone now, the big strong men of the Avenue
    Sonya's grandad, my father, those who knew each other
since short pants, handball alleys – when getting a job was more likely
    than anything and if you had a trade to your name
and your own box of tools, you were made

Eleanor Hooker

THE CONSOLATIONS OF SILENCE ARE FEW

Against that backdrop, she refuses the sign of peace –
nothing required but to shake hands, pray *Peace be with you* –
not even the lamps in this cold chapel are strong
enough to still her basilisk shadow.

Yoke-boned, she stands there, soundless, while our voices braid
over the warm solemn chord of a cello, not quietly,
unafraid of fumbling grief, of offering up our sign of peace.

And our dear friends in the front pews, a heap of sorrow,
recall their mother, her snow-drift hair, her grace, her
every goodness, her lately seasons bearing down to this.

Arriving one by one, they come, my failures to forgive –
carrying blackthorn sticks, sloe cudgels that
urge me to be unlike her, to drive my roots into the earth –
not to be afraid to come back deciduous as Oak or Ash,
to whisper, *Peace be with you*, to her back.

Greg Delanty

HIGH COUP

        A jet
        trails
        a line
of coke a c   r   o   s   s the sky's
        blue marble
        counter
        top

Greg Delanty

ON VIEWING *THE ROSES OF HELIOGABALUS*

The emperor and his hobnobbing retinue
        recline on the high dais. Everyone gazes
                up at them. He winks to his chosen few,
                        mutters "Watch this for a trap," hollers "Let's
                              play. Bring on the grand finale,"

downs his cup – a sign to drop the false ceiling of flowers
        on everybody below. You can feel
                nauseating petals catch in noses
                      and crying throats,
                            levels rapidly rising,
                                      drowning everyone in pink roses

Emily S Cooper

BABIES

we are considering franchising
or rather, not franchising

would it be a going concern or
as you like to call it
a growing concern

we construct concepts together
fusion foods like
the Indian/Italian tapas place
that I refuse to eat in

we come up with names
unrelated to our own heritages
a Sushi bar
called 'Papa Louis's Taverna'

we consider the costs of such a venture
the exhaustion the fatigue
the sleepless nights worrying
about reviews and profit margins

does the packed main street
really need another restaurant
even if we have faith in our own cuisine?

Mícheál McCann

LEAVING LONDON FOR BELFAST
   – for Andrew

Rather be parochial
than suitcase-weary
and tie-bonded
and slow to laugh
and desperate
to walk in the opposite direction,
quickly ...

Rather be coastal
than coughing,
slow in our going
than quiet with wanting.
Bless this plane, carrying
us over what we cannot swim.

My tired thighs hear
where we're going over the tannoy
and I can hear Jo Stafford
smiling as she sings. I missed you.
I hoak for a life vest under my seat
to realise I was wearing it all along.

Mícheál McCann

ÉTUDES

   1.

I'll go to concerts in the Ulster Hall
a few times a year to see the violin
soloists. My friends sense that
this is because I want to learn
fingerboard electric dashes of
the Shostakovich or the Barber
– nothing so heroic –
I go in the hope that something goes
wrong. The gold-plated E string
snapping mid-cadenza. An earring
slipping off, bouncing on the chin rest
then the floor *pop pop ... Bang*

– how these people can deal with disaster
at a moment's notice:

the string snapping in the middle
of a mournful B section of something
Tchaik-like

could I learn this, this coping?

   2. Photograph of Hallé Orchestra, 1901

A stage full of coat tails and
cocks between all of their legs
nestled like trapdoor spiders
but for one harpist, renowned
for her *dexterous*, impossibly
agile fingers, and *sensitive,
emotive playing*.

3. Urstudien

> *I have acceded to their request, in the hope that this publication will serve to improve not only the technic of my colleagues, but also their physical and moral well being so greatly depressed by the fear of failure.*
> – Carl Flesch

The central heating system
growls – no – rumbles
The house going to sleep my mother would say

and I am pressing and lifting
all four fingers in different chord
patterns to strengthen the muscles in my fingers

but I am struggling to anchor
my three fingers on intervals
while the index is active with *elastic surety*.

A strange drum-like singing
– my bow unsheathed –
as I'm trying to be quiet. My fingers collapse

under the pressure I place
on them, rightly. The washing
machine burps. We duet into the night.

4. Amateur Prayer

On a Sunday that is milky with undammed rain
I pick up my violin that wishes it remained a forest.

The soloists – so giant I decorate their ankles with
iron lanterns, that my children will remember them –

execute this piece precisely. I struggle to write
the word *perfectly*, unsure what it looks like. Content

is a word I'm prioritising as my fingers clump
like cheese over chords I cannot play. Sing a song.

Play, she'll say,
and toast our amateurism. It's the only thing we have left.

Lorna Shaughnessy

ERASURE
     – after Plein Air II *by Gerry Davis*

Faced with a blank canvas in your art class,
all you could think to paint was the bonfire
where you keep burning your past.
The flames still leap there, on the easel,
though the heat went out of it years ago
and you've been standing in the ashes too long;
the effort of keeping a shine on your shoes
is becoming too much.

You scarcely see yourself in the mirror these days
and you're aware you have begun to dress
like your mother in her Sunday best: suit, gloves, bag.
Time to open the clasp and see what's in there:
her lipstick, compact and cotton hankie, or the key
that will put you back behind the wheel?
There are those photographs of your son,
but best not look.

You sent money for a suit for the funeral
but only bits of him turned up. He moved
as if someone had taken an eraser to his limbs
and he couldn't connect with the ground
or feel a hand on his arm. There would be
no eye contact, even as you watched him leave.
Instead, he turned his head to look beyond
the canvas on your easel, outside the frame
of a once-shared past, its final pyre.

Paul Maddern

13 FRAGMENTS
   – *for Ciaran*

                a blackbird on the path when you arrived,
                          the spirit ushered inside

The bard of Glandore left us in the night
and our fields are flooded by endless rains.
There is great sadness today in Glandore.

                                  a blackbird,
                        descant to our keening

and the sky woman bears the weight of grief
and sings in a tongue we had forgotten
and we are shamed by her grief

                              the eclipsed sun,
                            the blackbird's eye

and tonight a great wind tears
through the streets of the Holyland
and we are all students of fear

                          so many scattered
                        we thought them crows:
                      a fusillade of blackbirds

and we mistook acceptance
in the horse's eye for sorrow

                      sunlight breaks and flickers –
                      the blackbird lifts, its shadow
                          short-lived on the page

and the Lagan has run dry and the bones
of the fording place are exposed

                              blackbird song
                                  is *the* air

and it is this
     and this is it
          a note let go

and we have not even begun to describe the blackbird

Tom French

CAST

– for Megumi Igarashi ('Rokudenashiko')

In the traditional way a death mask is cast
she has taken a cast of her vagina
with plaster of Paris that picks out perfectly
every tiny detail, every curve and crease.

*

Now judges pass sentence on Rokudenashiko
for casting a full-scale kayak from that cast
and paddling in that boat on open water
because they deem that craft to be obscene.

*

Because she sent the software to the cloud
for others with 3D printers to download
and print off copies of her lotus blossom,
she is even looking at time behind bars.

*

Rokudenashiko, in her speech from the dock,
declares she has learned to love her whole body
and to think no more nor less of her vagina
than of her arms and legs, her hands, her feet.

*

In the only image I have seen of her
she is handling her paddle like a pro
and looks to be giving birth to herself
in mid-stream in the middle of her life.

*

In the coracle I cast from my genitals and kneel
at the prow to row and name *The Happy Home*,
in the slipstream of Rokudenashiko's craft,
learning to love my whole body, I set sail.

John Kelly

LOCAL KNOWLEDGE

There are locals who would know
that when the pollan start to spawn,
a mighty fleet of pike migrates in hunger
from here to over there – to where
that hardly local yacht silhouettes itself
among seven wild islands – none of which
I can confidently name.

Say, for the sake of argument,
those two lads puttering past me now,
biting down hard on roll-your-owns
in their dirty, always-flooded boat –
you wouldn't know to look at them
but they have the measure of such marvels
as were known to Pliny,

Aristotle and Descartes –
that swallows overwinter underwater,
that eels come from mud,
that monkeys can talk if they want to
and that barnacle geese don't hatch from eggs
but grow instead on overhanging trees,
and are not birds at all but fish.

John Kelly

SPACE

When Mrs Adams tapped the blackboard
with a red fingernail and spoke of *space*

and why I must put *space* between my words,
all I could see were the planets and the stars –

Saturn's rings, crescent moons, the Milky Way,
Cassiopeia scratched and scraping up and down.

Cosmonauts floated like giant babies
between words like *Mum* and *Dad*,

Laika the mongrel yelped at the universe
between *dog* and *cat*, and elsewhere,

in the dusty nebulae of green and yellow chalk,
three American spacemen said their prayers,

pressed all the buttons in Apollo 13
and thought, tearfully, of home.

This morning as all the little stars,
newly formed in constellations,

lined out in Cabinteely Park
for their first competitive match,

I watched my son in his outsized jersey
chase a huge moon of a ball, and try

to make sense of yet more adult instruction –
the Mums and the Dads, the dogs on the pitch,

the coach shouting, *Space! Space!*
Take your time, buddy! You have space!

Simon Costello

THE LANDSLIDE

When the bones of the buried arrived
at our doors, no one was surprised.
The graveyard was shifting for months.

Everyone took to the streets, posting videos
of the Great Return.
An old principal arrived at the home
of his best student who'd never left town.

Late John McKew, known for his rendition
of 'Wild Rover' went head first through
the windscreen of a Garda car, while crossing
a road that hadn't been there in his lifetime.

Some locked their children in their rooms,
counsellors assessed the emotional damage.
Residents came, prodding the earth
with sticks, heaving in the churchyard.

I was the first to sink my hands earthwards,
finding you, like an undiscovered bomb.

Sharon Black

CAFÉ DES ARTS

What could be better at ten a.m.
than espresso, croissant and freshly pressed
orange juice at a table on rue St. Guilhem?

Somewhere else, big wheels are turning;
a factory worker is being fired,
an oil rig's sprung a leak,

a head of corporation is dabbing his wife's cheek
as she weathers a contraction:
eight billion lives revolving on their axles.

Here on St. Guilhem, an electric UPS van
glides between lit façades,
between a toddler in a pushchair

and a woman in red jeans with a matching caddy,
between two ladies with four dogs on leads
and a cyclist.

It meets a white van, reverses, pulls in to the side,
lets the petrol engine blather past.
Eight billion revolutions

in the time it takes to drink a coffee,
drain an orange juice, dab up buttery flakes,
the biggest then the smallest.

Sharon Black

HER HAIR

It rises as she cycles, a brown scarf
stitched to blonde, a stash of rippling
ice cream, a vanilla/coffee contrail.
It was postbox red then blue
before the colour lost itself
to shampoo, heat and ultraviolet. It lifts
at both sides, bleached strands
surging up like wings, or a flight path
more than bird or plane or angel.
She's flying down the street
like she's flying into life, feet off the pedals,
legs stuck out beneath the charity shop
skirt, flamingo socks and T bar Docs.
She wants to grow it to her ribs,
it hasn't been that long since she was twelve.
I want to run my fingers through it
but she'll never let me. Sometimes
when we hug, I turn in to her neck, inhale,
like I did when she was young, drinking
milky sweetness, heavier now
and tinged with sweat.
She ties it up in quick elastic
and blonde drizzles down like icing;
she knots it into space buns
and looks like her first teddy. But today
it's swaying free, she's off her bike
and leaning on a railing, looking at
the anchored yachts in the marina,
a tanker in the distance, the rocks
between the pier and quay, the breakers.

Tara Bergin

HOME-SCHOOLING

This is a test.
You need to listen to me.

The cherries' stalks have been removed.
I think this is the mice's hiding place.
Everyone's costumes are over there.
Now, show me the difference between
plural and *possessive*.

Listen to the instructions I'm about to give you.
Take all of the futures and turn them into pasts.

I want three sensible questions to the following answers.
Lydia's necklace. A stain. Twenty English pounds.

Larynx is to throat as vacuum is to ——.

Find the root of solitude.
It could be *positively phototropic*.

A trick.

When we say the birds are crying
do we mean that they are sad?

Tell me the truth. Keep talking.

One day I promise I will say:
This is the end of the test.

Nessa O'Mahony

IMAGINARY OCEANS, REAL SEALS

Pat Boran, *Then Again* (Dedalus Press, 2019), €12.50.
Moya Cannon, *Donegal Tarantella* (Carcanet Press, 2019), £9.99.
Patrick Deeley, *The End of the World* (Dedalus Press, 2019), €12.50.

Then Again, Pat Boran's seventh collection, explores the relationship between life and art, or rather the many attempts that artists make to capture a moment in time, and the many failures. Like Keats before him, Boran is fascinated by the eternal tension between the desire to capture experience and its inevitable frustration; try as we might, whatever the medium, we can never reproduce the essence of what we aim to represent. As with Keats's Grecian Urn, Boran's female figurines in the opening poem 'Stillness' ('Like two startled meerkats'), or the unseen breath of the couple photographed at the eponymous Baldoyle Race Meeting ('his solid, gruff uncertainty, her fragile, / dreamy elegance and grace'), can only approximate, not embody, that original experience. But the poet has long accepted that approximation is our best attempt to capture the 'unnameable thing' described in the poem 'Roundabout'; that 'unidentified miracles', as he suggests in the poem of the same title, can be found in the least expected places (in this case 'the low steel basin' of a back garden).

Galleries and museums provide the inspiration for many of the poems, and many allow Boran to demonstrate a very Keatsian negative capability: an ability to imagine oneself into other lives preserved through art. His 'Common Heron', first espied in the Natural History Museum, breathes again here, 'entranced, intent, / reading the curving lines / in the wood of my case'. That the art of the taxidermist is no less that of the writer is suggested through the transformation of the bird's beak into something more writerly:

> but my bill's steely tip
> is still steady,
> still poised at the ink-well of night,
> still ready to dip.

That nocturnal ink-well is a familiar trope in Boran's work. As a younger poet, he roamed the squares of Georgian Dublin and captured the nighttown in all its flawed glory. He evokes that period again in the poem 'Robert', an elegy for a writer who died by his own hand; that frailty of our hold on life is expressed in short, almost tortured 3-syllable lines, and provokes this urgent reminder of our duty to each other:

> Thanks, I owe
> you, we po-
> ets must stand
> each for each
> must look out
> for each ot-
> her be twice
> what we are
> on our own

Memory is another form of artistic expression; we constantly reshape experience in our effort to recapture it. Boran explicitly ties in remembered life and art, and doffs another, this time explicit, cap to the apothecary poet in two poems. 'The Way Things Are' is a memory of young men out on the town – 'moments later, / we'd all be out, everyone together, / dazed and wasted and starting the recriminations'; in 'Greek Vase', their exploits are transmuted into art as Boran imagines the fighters immortalised 'like old friends / reuniting, like drunks lunging / when the last bar closes'.

These poems range from Dublin to Paris, to Sicily and Cyprus, to sports-fields and libraries, and include elegies for dead friends and fellow poets such as Philip Casey and Dennis O'Driscoll, in language that is always precise, imagistic, authentic, narrative-driven, and with a strong ear for dialogue. There is a recognition of the need to simply 'see'. '"Give me the eye, for I love the eye,"' says his father's neighbour in 'The Pig's Eye', and Boran continues to put that honest, Keatsian eye to good work.

If Boran's poetry shares preoccupations with the younger generation of Romantic poets, Moya Cannon's lyric sensibility would not be out of place in Wordsworth's circle, for whom landscape and the natural world remain the ultimate source both of inspiration and consolation. This is Cannon's sixth collection, and once again we experience the sublime in her renderings of places near and far. The poem 'At Three Castles Head We Catch Our Breath' gives a flavour of how she manages to make language swoop and dive as it captures the numinous:

> A flat, faulted slab of cliff soars
> and shimmers far above us
> then slants far below,
> into a young ocean
> we call the Atlantic.

That 'faulted' so cleverly makes us see 'vaulted', yet retains the geological specificity she is exploring here. Or what about the exquisite portrait of three seals in 'A Three-Seal Morning', with 'noses up / near a round of stones and seaweed', who –

> lean forward, faces at a concert –
> a long, clicking stone-ripple –
> then, gently, fall back.

Imaginary oceans, real seals. Time and again the reader gasps at the just so-ness of Cannon's descriptions, her ability to find an adjective that captures the essence of something whilst making us look at it anew. Never more so than in the poems set in her beloved Connemara, an area so anthologised, so captured in poetry and paintings that it would seem impossible to conjure up anything new to say, yet here she is describing The Twelve Bens in the poem of the same name:

> yesterday morning, striding
> in their shawls of rain and, later,
> sun-blasted, and today
> dappled under running clouds.

So far, so Paul Henry, you might say, but then Cannon shifts up a gear, arguing that we love them not just for their aesthetic, but for their mood, their 'companionability'. Never again will I see those mountains without thinking first of Cannon's companionable peaks.

It can be hard to separate landscape from the history that sometimes mars it, and in this collection, Cannon explores this idea both at home and abroad, seeking traces of those whose lives, and stories, have been obliterated from the official narrative. In 'October 1945', a distraught mother seeks traces of her daughter killed by the Hiroshima bombing, finding 'under a melted bottle – her daughter's / scorched wooden sandal', whilst in 'Mal'ta Boy, 22,000 BC', she wonders 'how many moons' his mother wept for the boy whose bones were preserved: 'the rickle of a four-year-old child's bones, / found under a stone slab / by a lake in eastern Siberia.'

These 'fallen sparrows' of history, as she calls them in this poem, appear elsewhere in the book. So too do the women edited out of the official narrative in the first place. In 'The Countermanding Order, 1916', she reminds us of the mothers, sisters, and daughters, all of whom had their own experiences of those crucial moments in history:

> And my young grandmother,
> what of her?
> Was she, too, dejected?
> No documentary evidence exists.

The title poem, 'Donegal Tarantella', offers important reminders for those suspicious of sea-borne migrants and who think that culture is only indigenous:

> Tunes wash up, ocean-polished pebbles,
> in the kitchens of south Donegal –
> mazurkas, germans, highlands, hornpipes, jigs, reels,
> all gone native since they were washed in
> by waves of returning emigrants,
> Napoleonic garrisons,
> travelling pipers or fiddling tinsmiths.

This beautiful collection ends as it opens, with glorious vistas of our geological past in the poem 'Climb' where, in a nod to Heaney's 'Postscript', we see 'Below, a hundred islands come and go – / doors of perception blow open, blow closed.'

So where might Patrick Deeley's seventh collection, *The End of The World*, fit into the self-imposed straitjacket of Romantic corollaries I've been proposing here? Perhaps Shelley's political anger might come nearest to matching Deeley's consciousness of the interconnectedness of human experience in the face of our apparent thirst for self-annihilation. In the italicised poem that prefaces the book and gives it its title, Deeley provides a bleak context in which to link the death of a young cyclist in Harold's Cross to a displaced Sumatran tribesman:

> *... both haunt us, being more than props*
>
> *for pathos, more than backdrops to the uselessness*
> *even of beauty in face of greed or misfortune.*
> *The end of the world is happening*

Yet there are alternatives, Deeley argues, were nature allowed to pursue its own course. In 'The Ash Pit', he asks us to 'Imagine, just imagine' if 'nature could allow for its own design'; in the next poem, 'Two Hundred Million Animals', he further reminds us of the 'two hundred million animals we kill for sport / each year'. There are regular references to the world 'burning down, being / blown down, withering, drowning' ('Scribble Lark') interposed with poems where nature does, indeed, allow for its own design yet, even then, cannot avoid a more malign plan. In 'The Migration', he recalls:

> Once ever did I see the eels go on a belly march,
> teems of them 'splathering' across the wet
> Callows, homing to the seaweed of the Sargasso.

Even here, however, they risked human capture, destruction: 'It sizzled, / / it hopped and shrivelled and died hard.' Those same Callows housed other portents, the eponymous 'half-carcass of calf' wavering 'below the fried-egg scum' showing once more how 'barbarity shadows the loveliness / always, tricked up in the clotted primordial' ('Half-carcass of Calf'). But the Callows also provide escape, as in 'My Mother's Getaway', where 'She'd go / morning or evening to the nurture / of not thinking, her feet swishing'. The coin is always double-sided in Deeley's poetry; capture and escape seem inextricably linked. The solution is to endure, as the migrants in 'Towards a Frontier' remind us: 'Our feet are rude. They endure. Our hearts are set / on living through what we suffer.'

The final of the book's four sections returns back to nature, and natural encounters, a needed reminder that despite the imminence of destruction, there are proofs of survival going back millennia. The poem 'Precursor' imagines the Valentia Island tetrapod's first steps on land – 'Tetrapod, four-foot, accurate but basic / / as the mud in my mind's eye / you are plodding'; whilst, in 'Toad', that creature's hoary ancestors 'crouched / under tarpaulin of leathery wing-webbing' give a clue to how we might all be saved: 'your muddling through, your survival'. And failing that, there is still, as the poem 'However the Malady' suggests:

>   ... this play of light, the end of it
> a ramble along streets to a dwindling path where two
> trout leap in the Dodder as it dandles the glow
> of the bit moon – tipping its hat, say, to me and you.

Small consolation, perhaps, but for twenty-first-century Romantics, as good as it gets.

Benjamin Keatinge

A VAST FIDELITY

Frank Ormsby, *The Rain Barrel* (Bloodaxe Books, 2019), £12.
Enda Coyle-Greene, *Indigo, Electric, Baby* (Dedalus Press, 2020), €12.50.
Peter Sirr, *The Gravity Wave* (The Gallery Press, 2019), €11.95.

In his appraisal of two critical books on the Northern Irish Troubles, Peter Sirr (writing in the *TLS* in 1998) warns against a default 'critical expectation that Northern poets will shine their lamps on the "troubles"'. This cautionary suggestion is important in reading the poetry of Frank Ormsby whose poetic career has spanned the Troubles without being subsumed by them. The concluding poem of his 1977 collection, *A Store of Candles*, evokes a domestic storeroom containing such innocuous items as:

> ... a spare fire-bar;
>
> the shaft of a broom; a tyre; assorted nails;
> a store of candles for when the light fails.
>   – 'UNDER THE STAIRS'

Domesticity – the routines of family, work, and everyday life – is also integral to subsequent collections, notably: *The Ghost Train* (1995), *Fireflies* (2009), and *Goat's Milk: New and Selected Poems* (2015). References to violence in Northern Ireland have tended to be occasional and oblique so that, for example, a poem like 'Helen' from *The Ghost Train* places 'The war' in the background to the more central event of the birth of the poet's daughter:

> The war will soon be over, or so they say.
> Five floors below the Friday rush-hour starts.
> You're out and breathing. We smile to hear you cry.
> Your long fingers curl around our hearts.

Of course, Frank Ormsby has been a key figure in Irish poetry circles for many years, not least as editor of *The Honest Ulsterman* from 1969 to 1989, and as editor of such important anthologies as *A Rage for Order: Poetry of the Northern Irish Troubles* (Blackstaff Press, 1992). Such important literary projects and roles have unavoidably entailed a shining of lamps onto the political violence of the times. But Michael Longley rightly reminds us, in his introduction to Ormsby's *New and Selected Poems*, that 'Few people have done more for poetry' even in difficult times and, alongside his own poetry, this wider dedication compels our admiration. It is fitting then that Ormsby's achievement should be fully recognised by his appointment as Ireland Professor of Poetry, and that full attention can be given to his own work and its relation to what Longley describes as 'that extraordinary generation of Northern Irish poets which includes Ciaran Carson, Medbh McGuckian, Paul Muldoon and Tom Paulin'.

What is most noteworthy about the poems in *The Rain Barrel* is the extent to which they evoke a pre-lapsarian Ulster inflected through the poet's origins in rural Enniskillen. Loss of innocence and the vexed legacy of the conflict are inflected via a number of poems about the missing, including 'The Disappeared' ('lost graves on the mountain'), 'Winter Landscape with Searchers' ('a seminar on loss'), and 'There Will Be a Knock' ('She checks the mail every day for his handwriting'). But such sombre poems are counterbalanced by more homely recollections. The collection's opening poem 'Untroubled' recalls the year 1962 with the schoolboy-poet doing his homework on a 'quiet night' where only 'a dog in the hills' disturbs the peaceful scene. 'The Rain Barrel' itself is a symbol of continuity, 'a family emblem' that survives the upheavals of intervening decades until finally its 'hoops loosen' and it has 'to be dismantled'. As such, it is an emblem of endurance and testimony to the non-sectarian thread of daily life which 'never comes to bloodshed' despite being 'soaked in experience'.

These poems of innocence and experience resonate with those of another member of that 'extraordinary generation', Seamus Heaney, whose poem 'A Sofa in the Forties' captures that uneasy atmosphere of rural seclusion in pre-Troubles Ulster characterised by 'history and ignorance'. Indeed, the central trope of Heaney's poem (from *The Spirit Level*, 1996) is that of a childhood game of trains revolving round a family sofa. But in the context of World War II, then in progress, the capacity of the children to 'be transported' takes on a terrible double-meaning that brings history and ignorance into direct alignment. Heaney's poem asks 'Ghost-train? Death-gondola?', just as Ormsby's own poem 'The Ghost Train' considers 'a mass grave', 'cholera victims', and 'more immediate shades', also in the context of 'children's futures'. It is thus unsurprising that the poems of *The Rain Barrel* should worry at the contours of history, innocence, and ignorance, and that the troubling images 'of the disappeared' ('Winter Landscape with Searchers') should be set against the reassurances of everyday objects ('The Rain Barrel', 'Some Farmyard Buckets'), nature ('The Kingfisher', 'Starlings'), and family ('Seaside', 'Parents'). A master of the haiku and of the short poem, Ormsby creates poignant vignettes of friends and family who have '"gleamed and are gone"' ('Towards an Elegy'), and the shade of Seamus Heaney is honoured 'in a shy courtesy of loss' in three short and moving tributes ('With Seamus Heaney in Mind').

As Ciaran Carson famously wrote in his review of Heaney's *North* in *The Honest Ulsterman* (1975), 'No one really escapes from the massacre', and indeed, Ormsby surveys more than one vista of violence and history in his poetry (*A Northern Spring*, for example, examines issues of memory in connection with World War II and the stationing of Allied troops in Northern Ireland in the latter stages of that war). These scrupulous new poems reaffirm Ormsby's 'vast fidelity' to poetry itself ('He Was the Eighth to Go Missing'), a commitment that has now movingly transcended the daily assaults on the senses during the years of violence. They meditate on the fidelity of 'mourners' to their loved ones, but at the same time they also celebrate small and large 'pleasures' ('Small Things') as well as 'innocence' ('Cows 1'), and those many innocuous things that did indeed escape from the massacre.

Enda Coyle-Greene's third collection – *Indigo, Electric, Baby* – contains a range of brilliantly-orchestrated poems brought together around the trope of the colour blue and its cognates: 'indigo', 'cerulean, cyan, / cobalt, navy, manganese' ('Indigo, Electric, Baby'). The volume alludes to the visual arts in complex ways (an epigraph by poet and art historian Thomas MacGreevy is taken from his 1929 poem 'Gloria de Carlos V', which in turn evokes Titian's *La Gloria* in the Prado, Madrid, itself a complex, colour-coded, religious painting). Although not mentioned explicitly by Coyle-Greene, Picasso's 'blue period' may also figure in these equations, and Picasso is mentioned in MacGreevy's poem. Such speculations could further deflect us in the direction of Wallace Stevens' meditative masterpiece 'The Man with the Blue Guitar', with its linkage to Picasso's 1904 painting, 'The Old Guitarist'.

However, none of this is needed to enjoy Coyle-Greene's technical virtuosity and musical precision which are much in evidence in this collection. Indeed, music – 'The nuances of the blue guitar', in Stevens' phrase – might be said to be the more important sister art here with the central sequence 'The Blue Album – Eleven Small Self-Songs' structured around specific songs and pieces, classical and modern, which are listed in the Notes to the book. 'Self-Song 1' takes its inspiration from Schubert's 'An die Musik', recalling:

> An empty landing in a Georgian house.
> A quiet child, too much so.
> My mother's voice: soprano,
> *mezzo*.

In 'Self-Song 2', the apprehensive child:

> ... choose[s] small stones to skip
> across a universe of drifts;
>
> mapped by a splash, each
> stows a story all its own ...

There are, one suspects, interiorities at play here, always suggestive, if not always immediately accessible. Walter Pater argued, in his *The Renaissance: Studies in Art and Poetry* (1873), that 'All art constantly aspires towards the condition of music', and in some of Coyle-Greene's poems, the music can be enjoyed for its own melody alone. But Pater's nugget of wisdom only goes so far and there is plenty of content here amplified by an exquisite mastery of form. 'A Sky Full of Noise' is a 'self-song' perhaps connected to Susan Cain's book *Quiet: The Power of Introverts in a World That Can't Stop Talking* (2013) that Coyle-Greene mentions in an interview on the occasion of the publication of her second collection *Map of the Last* (2013). The poem is dialogic within the self, and considers the virtues of a measured withdrawal from the 'noise' of the world:

> there's a sky full of noise
> as the flight path to and from
> this city won't shut up.
>
> Yes, yes, I intend to mention
> this, that, whatever –
> maybe when I get the guts
> to let you know how much
> we need to speak,
> I might.
>   – 'A SKY FULL OF NOISE'

Via Shakespeare, the poet adapts the language of Caliban by using the artistry of Ariel or Prospero. Such dramatic parallels remind us that poems are often performances and their mise-en-scène serve to reference many situations – past experiences, psychological states and/or historical events (Coyle-Greene's remarkable poem 'Salvage', from *Map of the Last*, about the sinking of the *Tayleur* off the north Dublin coast in 1854 is a fine example of the last category). In this new collection, the well-wrought sestina 'Power Cut' grips the reader through linguistic variations of 'power', 'cut', 'walls', 'house', 'garden', 'left' to convey details of a domestic and residential drama the poetic 'zigzags' of which are conveyed with wit and concision. Awkward social situations also feature in 'Bruise' and 'Underground', poems that use the intimacy and anonymity of the modern city to speculate on the lives of people 'we will never know'.

This sense of isolation can be traced elsewhere, in the disorientations of 'a plane full of strangers' ('If, in Moving'), for example, or the disquieting 'phone in the hall' of 'That Blue Time'. Nevertheless, even with these acknowledgements of vulnerability, and the fear that we are 'frangible as glass', the poems retain a hard-won sense of renewal and trust, a belief that ultimately 'People are kind' ('That Blue Time') and that it is imperative to rejoice in 'driving / this song's piano-cascade chorus / with my loudest voice' ('The Blue Album'). *Indigo, Electric, Baby* is an accomplished collection, full of music.

Peter Sirr's latest collection *The Gravity Wave* exhibits a thematic eclecticism which occupies poetic territories his readers will, by now, know and recognise. The title refers to a phenomenon in physics, 'disturbances in the curvature of spacetime', as Wikipedia helpfully informs us. Such spatio-temporal particularities are referenced in the collection's title poem, but also in the treatment of time and space in several other key poems. 'Inheritances' refers to 'the zeptosecond' (which is a tiny slice of time, a fraction of a second) 'where our silences collide', and 'The Gravity Wave' dwells upon: 'the micron's micron, the hair's breadth's whisper / of what passed between us.' Yet, several of these poems collate different time perspectives, from the zeptosecond, to the day-to-day, to generational time (the human life span), to historical and mythological time. For example, an everyday circumstance of 'Walking Home' prompts a series of time-shifts that move the poem across vast temporal realms:

> ... the centuries hang like apples on the trees,
> unkillable wattle, unending stone, every morsel, every bone.
>
> If there's a beginning, a first, awkward stumbling to the clearing,
> a difficult but finally successful fording of the river, if the ash pit
>
> opens, the skulls cavort, the myths crawl back from the woods

We sense here the Vikings of Wood Quay or the earliest settlements of Dublin and these imaginative leaps leave the poet 'bewildered, somehow comforted' taking 'the long way home' ('Walking Home'). There is a questing intelligence at work here resembling that of the mapmaker in Sirr's 2014 collection *The Rooms* who wants 'to stand at the centre / of a great clutter' to provide 'an infinite census' of the world ('The Mapmaker's Song'). But in these new poems, Sirr is obliged to desist in the endeavour to record each zeptosecond, and several poems chart Sirr's attempt to hold on to the essential within the flux of time. 'The Now Slice' moves from the breakfast table back to the 'Mycenaean' era as if moving in a time capsule, returning to a world 'of toast and cats' where 'the future will already be over'. Meanwhile, 'Blackbird' finds the poet-speaker 'Possessed with what must outlive you', finding comfort in 'The blackbird' who 'sings *tomorrow, tomorrow, tomorrow* / to the fading laptop, the empty room'.

All of this adds to the impression, articulated in 'Radio Life', that we inhabit 'a museum of obsolescence' on personal, historical, and technological planes. Even though the poet wishes, on occasion, to 'let the technologies rot' and to privilege personal happiness, what is discomforting is how the human and the mechanical in fact live side by side 'obsolescing' together ('Radio Life'). Yet, as the radio waves glide through the air and the poet listens to a loved one, 'A light flares, your voice comes on / as if a great switch has been thrown', so that the radio becomes a bringer of life, and the oppositions of science and art, machine and human, are no longer even viable. In this, Sirr draws on previous poetic explorations of technology, such as his poem 'The Beautiful Engines' from *Bring Everything* (2000) which concludes:

> it would have been terrible to miss:
> an engine released at last from its name
> to flicker like lightning in the brain,
> the valves of the planet looming through glass ...

... and where the lucky chance of the poet's email at the Irish Writers' Centre (IWC) mirroring that of the Irish Wildbird Conservancy (IWC) led to him receiving daily information about 'king eider', 'scarlet rosefinch', 'Baird's sandpiper', 'wagtails on the north slob' all 'flocking in daily error to [his] computer' ('The Beautiful Engines'). Thus the impersonal images of 'the planet looming through glass' or of the 'micron's micron' of the zeptosecond take on a colour and beauty of their own, illuminations which this latest collection skilfully curates.

This scientific curiosity is joined by Sirr's ethical seriousness in poems like 'Add to Dictionary' (about the war in Syria) and 'Haus der Wansee-Konferenz' (set at the location where the 'Final Solution' was planned by the Nazis), but readers will also enjoy the intertextual playfulness and dexterity of less sombre poems. The ekphrastic 'Bruegel: The Wedding in the Barn' (first published in *Lines of Vision: Irish Writers on Art*, 2014), delineates the buffoonery presented in Bruegel's painting in terms of a contemporary TV soap opera:

> ... This one's had it,
> his head slumped on the table,
> hell is a furious music.

[. . .]

>   ... The fat
> peasant lunges at the cameraman.
> Bruegel sighs: the ratings are up
> but the complaints are pending.

And music features more seriously in 'The Conversation', dedicated to Martin Hayes and David Power, and in 'Winterreise'; meanwhile, German literary heritage is referenced, for example, in 'Kleist's Grave' and 'Blue Octavo: Images from Kafka'. Sirr's thematic and linguistic range, his crossing of cultural and disciplinary boundaries, is the signal facet of his art. If the volume lacks a unifying set of concerns, it retains what Patricia Craig has called 'a quietly cryptic quality' and 'dreamlike composure', which give tonal fluency to what is an expansive and fascinating collection.

Nicholas Grene

STILLED MOVEMENT

Ciaran Carson, *Still Life* (The Gallery Press, 2019), €11.95.
Paul Muldoon, *Frolic and Detour* (Faber and Faber, 2019), £14.99 hb.

Still Life: the book's title is a brave and resonant pun. Some of the seventeen paintings that act as prompts for the poems in Ciaran Carson's volume are actual still lives – like Angela Hackett's *Lemons on a Moorish Plate* – but most are not. The wonderfully moving secondary significance of the phrase is the assertion of the poet, diagnosed with terminal cancer, that he is still alive, still experiencing the sheer plenitude of being alive. And the recurrent preoccupation of the book is the way both painting and poetry capture the continuous movement of life, stilling it into form. As a last testament collection, it would bring home to any admirer of Carson's work the sense of bereavement in his loss. But it is much more than that: a bold new experiment in writing as much as a heroic gesture in the face of death.

One of the influences on *Still Life*, as Carson makes clear in his concluding acknowledgements, was TJ Clark's *The Sight of Death*. Clark's 'experiment in art writing', as he subtitled the book, was a journal devoted entirely to the contemplation of just two Poussin paintings. Poussin figures centrally in *Still Life*, including the two paintings at the centre of Clark's study, *Landscape with a Calm*, and *Landscape with a Man Killed by a Snake*. But Carson does not confine himself to the examination and response to the pictures that provide the titles for the poems. Instead, each image serves, like Canaletto's *The Stonemason's Yard*, as a 'palimpsest to write upon'. The paintings move in and out of Carson's journal, which takes in his daily walks round North Belfast with his wife Deirdre, recollections of their life together as fellow musicians, visits to the hospital for chemotherapy, memories of some of the terrible events of the Troubles of the 1970s.

More or less free association of sights and sounds takes Carson away from the evocation of Monet or Velázquez, William Nicholson or Yves Klein. (No paintings from before the Renaissance figure in the poems; it is a gallery divided between Old Masters, going back to Patinir in the early sixteenth century, up to contemporary pictures owned by the poet himself, like the beautiful Jeffrey Morgan, *Hare Bowl*, which is reproduced on the book's cover. Within that range Carson seems equally at home with the representational and the abstract, classical and modern). Directed by the art history he reads to analyse the materials the artists use, Carson gives the same self-conscious attention to the language and form of his poetry, even as he writes it. The semantics and morphology of words are scrutinised: as a nurse eases in the needle for his drip treatment he reflects:

> ... *Cannula* the Latin
> for a little reed,
> Or maybe a pen – the needle a nib with chemo ink to overwrite
> the faulty DNA.
> – 'JEFFREY MORGAN, *HARE BOWL*, 2008'

He remembers how his signature long line (first adopted in *The Irish For No*) filled the width of a typescript A4 page. But in print the stanza form has a quite different visual effect:

> the landscape
> Format of the stanza radically changes shape, becoming
> more like a tree
> Or a shrub with a dense central trunk – arboreal, in other
> words, like these
> Which you are viewing now, which I have written
> only now.
> – 'JOACHIM PATINIR, *LANDSCAPE WITH SAINT JEROME*, 1516-17'

The long lines and the capacious stanzas of variable length – seven, eight, ten, even fourteen lines – enable Carson to include the most variable materials: prose extracts from art historical writing; comments and asides; direct addresses to Deirdre, his constant companion through the poems, as well as the precise evocation of the paintings. The contemplation of a picture by Gerard Dillon, in which three different images of the artist appear in completely different attitudes and picture planes, speaks for Carson himself: 'here I am this that and the other' ('Gerard Dillon, *Self Contained Flat*, exhibited 1955'). It is simultaneously an assertion of the unity and the shiftingness of the speaker, the artist, the poet. As paintings can hold heterogeneous figures in formal relationship, Carson's poems still into form the apparently random agglomerations of thoughts and feelings in the day by day musings of the journal. We are constantly reminded of how fully Carson lived in the world, with his intense and learned appreciation of visual art, his musicianship, his loving attention to the most mundane details of his surroundings. We watch all this come into life, taking shape in the poems, with the heartbreaking knowledge that this animated presence – 'here I am this that and the other' – is no longer there.

Happily, Paul Muldoon is still very much with us, and with *Frolic and Detour* is as quirky, as brilliantly inventive, and as unblinking as ever in the contemplation of the brutalities of history. He has two poems which are given painting titles, 'Pablo Picasso: *Bottle of Bass and Glass* (1914)', and 'Georges Braque: *Still Life with Bottle of Bass*'. (Picasso and Braque drank Bass?) But they do not take off from the images as in Carson's ekphrastic sequence. Instead, the Cubist bottles of Bass inspire a playful, witty fantasia on the drinking habits of past writers – 'Dante Alighieri drank it straight no chaser / Even though he talked in circles he never stood his round' – with possible and impossible drinking companions: 'John Milton drank with Edna St Vincent Millay'. And when we move on from Picasso to Braque, we get exactly the same poem word for word, only the titles being different. The two paintings are quite different but when it comes to writers' inspiration, 'You could say we all drank from the same vessel', Pierian spring or bottle of Bass.

Carson's journal format chronicles, moment by moment, the rush of writing that animated the last six months of his life. Muldoon's poems were created over a longer span of time, and many of them were commissioned for particular occasions. 2016, at the centre of Ireland's Decade of Centenaries, elicited several of these. So, evenhandedly, there are World War I poems, 'July 1, 1916: With the Ulster Division', 'Wilfred Owen: November 4, 1918' and 'Armistice Day', to balance out '1916: The Eoghan Rua Variations', one of the outstanding commemorations of the Rising. The starting point are the four lines in Irish attributed to the eighteenth-century Eoghan Rua Ó Súilleabháin, an 'ubi sunt' reflection on the transitoriness of power. In his time, Ó Súilleabháin, contemplating the deaths of world conquerors Alexander and Caesar, the destruction of Tara and Troy, consoles himself with the prospect that the English too will be gone one day: 'na Sasanaigh féin do b'fhéidir go bhfaighidís bás'. At the end of each of the nine sonnets that make up Muldoon's poem, we return to a different version of Ó Súilleabháin's lines:

> Now the world's been brought low. The wind's heavy with soot.
> Alexander and Caesar. All their retinue.
> We've seen Tara buried in grass, Troy trampled underfoot.
> The English? Their days are numbered, too.

Where Yeats's refrain clanged out at the end of each section of 'Easter 1916', saluting the epoch-making event just as it had happened, Muldoon looks back from the distance of a hundred years at what, for Eoghan Rua, was only a Utopian prospect. The conventional story of the Rising – 'On Easter Monday I was still en route / from Drumcondra to the GPO' – is given in characteristic Muldoonian terms as 'a dispute / between a starch-shirt cuckoo / and a meadow-pipit'. But underpinned by the Eoghan Rua threnody in all its variations and the *longue durée* of the historical perspective, there is no triumphalism in commemorating the dispossession of the dispossessing English cuckoo.

Carson's free play of image association is held only by the form of the chosen long line and the stanza. For Muldoon, quite as free playing and associative as his fellow Ulster poet, there is also the fixative of rhyme and the exigencies of complex poetic structures. '*Encheiresin Naturae*' – the title a technical alchemical term for the manipulation of nature drawn from Goethe's *Faust* – is a so-called 'crown of sonnets', a sequence of fifteen linked poems. They all follow the correct rhyme scheme for a Petrarchan sonnet, but with the last word of each poem picked up as the concluding word of the first line of the next, the 'g' rhyme of one reappearing as the 'a' rhyme of its successor. Muldoon lets himself off the full demands of the 'heroic crown', which requires each of the fourteen lines of the final sonnet to repeat the first lines of the other fourteen in successive order. He contents himself with ending each of lines 2-14 of the last poem with the final words of sonnets 1-13 in order. Within this intricate filigree of sound and sense, there is an extraordinary diversity of interconnected images and ideas threaded around grain: sowing, reaping, threshing, in Egypt, in Ireland, in India.

Muldoon has always been very conscious of Native American history and the horrors of the colonial process by which the peoples of the continent were destroyed. Two of the poems, 'In the Field with Mangas Coloradas', and 'With Joseph Brant in Canojoharie', focus on Native American leaders who fought for the colonisers – Mangas for the Americans, Brant for the British – and were subsequently betrayed. References to the atrocities of the Indian Mutiny (or first War of Independence, depending on your viewpoint), memories of the Holocaust or of the dead babies in 'At Tuam', let no-one off the hook of history. 'It Wasn't Meant to Be Like This' contrasts the futuristic optimism of the 1960s with the contemporary present, 'When we stared into the abyss'. Most moving of all is the desolate ballad 'Corncrake and Curlew'. It looks as if it is going to be an environmental lament for the all but disappeared corncrake: 'The corncrake ratchets up the odds / of being cut down in the aftermath.' But gestures to 'an execution squad', 'crates of rifles and rifle clips', which intersperse the vignettes of old-style farming, bring us out to the haunting final stanza:

> The corncrake marvels at the land being green
> although the hay's been saved.
> The curlew knows the land's so green
> because it's a mass grave.

Sombre and disquieting as so many of these poems are, Muldoon's wit and self-mockery constantly enliven the experience of reading this book. There is the splendid 'Position Paper', using as epigraph a particularly fractured and obfuscating quotation from Donald Trump, and consisting of a whole nonsense sequence of garbled traditional sayings: 'One rotten apple keeps the doctor away. / When the doctor's away the cat will get the cream.' In the densest and most digressive title poem, 'Frolic and Detour', Muldoon remarks tongue in cheek: 'I'd just as soon not be sidetracked / by further allusions to popular culture'. Detours there are in plenty throughout this poem and all the others in the collection, but frolic? There has to be conscious irony in the use of such a frivolously playful term from a poet who is always playful but seldom frivolous.

These two books serve to underline how different intertextuality has become for the poet – and the reviewer – in the time of the internet. The ricochet of words, images, and ideas that has been a staple of poetry since the onset of modernism, now travels out into the ethersphere and back. Carson may have been initially looking at reproductions of paintings in books, memories of seeing them in galleries, but he (like the reader reviewing his poems) can call them up from Google, move in on details down to the last pixelated magnification. Muldoon's 'Hunting with Eagles, Western Mongolia, 2016' can be tracked back to its source, an online article by David Stamboulis, which has as a 'related story' at the bottom of the website screen, 'Why Genghis Khan's Tomb can't be found': Genghis Khan's tomb also features in the poem. Apparently miscellaneous materials, gathered from both actual and virtual worlds, dance to the poets' tunes, are held within their shaped poetic forms.

Matthew Rice

CURFUFFLES

Scott McKendry, *Curfuffle* (The Lifeboat Press, 2019), £6.50.
Caitlin Newby, *Ceremony* (The Lifeboat Press, 2019), £6.50.
Grace Wilentz, *Holding Distance* (Green Bottle Press, 2019), £6.
Louise G Cole, *Soft Touch* (smith|doorstop, 2019), £7.50.

Belfast's The Lifeboat Press, run by Manuela Moser and Stephen Connolly, is a small publishing house that is rapidly belying its size. Scott McKendry's debut pamphlet, *Curfuffle*, is an example of this, having been selected as the Poetry Book Society's Autumn Pamphlet Choice in 2019. McKendry's North Belfast roots are lovingly invoked throughout, although not without a level of ambivalence that is fascinating to behold as it adds to the charge of the language he employs. As in 'Fiesta', a poem that tells of three mates settling down to watch *Sea of Love* on DVD, before a group of masked men bursts in to commandeer their car in order to commit a sectarian murder, with one left behind to 'mind' the trio: 'he ... asked what film we'd been watching. "The *Sea of Love*", // I told him. ... "Oh ... put it back on, isita good one?" / I mind snapping: "Seemed deadon till youse cunts came."'

The dialect McKendry uses is faithful to the area in which he grew up, and it is fresh and appealing to see it utilised to such great effect, providing punch and lending weight to the late John Hurt's insistence, when discussing the film *44 Inch Chest*, that swearing can be an art form when used correctly. Consider the following from the penultimate poem 'Belphégor, Lord of the Gap, Hell's Ambassador to France': 'and you'd be *cootchie-woo coochie-wootchie-cooing* a sloth; / or feeding bits of Red Leicester and pickle to a hungry harpy eagle // from a bumbag slung over a branch. And I, Belphégor, would be / egging you on. "Go on, love," I'd say, "that's fucking ingenious."' It's the alliterative pleasure of 'hungry', harpy', 'bumbag', branch', Belphégor', that makes the swear word when it eventually arrives so satisfying.

It takes skill to swagger through a poetic form while still displaying the necessary control that sets it off, and also, perhaps, not a little nerve. McKendry is reaching into himself and deciding that this is him, this is how he speaks, and what's wrong with putting that into poetry. He has recently completed a Ph.D. at Queen's University, Belfast, and the academic filter, perhaps, is best utilised when channelling that raw experience. There is also fun to be had with politics from further afield, and in the historical, via recollections of primary school in the excellent 'Greasepaint', a poem that puts a whole new spin on Muldoon's 'Anseo':

> How Carl Marks got through seven years of primary school
> without a raised eyebrow, never mind sniggering, at roll call
>
> God only knows.

This reviewer was laughing out loud in a coffee shop when reading this, and was more than happy to field questions from my server as to why. That being said, the 'fun' never strays too far from the 'serious', which is a point impossible to ignore when reading *Curfuffle*; this is where its power lies.

Throughout the collection, we can see shades of Martin Mooney, Tom Paulin, and Paul Muldoon, which is a compliment to McKendry's blended wit. Also, to this reviewer's mind at least, the now all-too-apt ghostly presence of the late and much missed Ciaran Carson and Padraic Fiacc (the former having been a mentor and friend to the young poet). Having said this, McKendry has honed a style that is distinctly his own, and having been the recipient of the most recent Patrick Kavanagh Award, along with the aforementioned PBS selection, it is refreshing to see the poetry world concurring. This is a debut chock full of originality.

Caitlin Newby was shortlisted for *The White Review*'s poetry prize in 2018, and on this evidence it is easy to see why. Her debut pamphlet, *Ceremony*, also from the Lifeboat stable, is equally as thrilling as *Curfuffle*, albeit tonally different in its emotional scope and depth. The very title of the pamphlet is remarkable in itself, in that we tend to associate the word 'ceremony' with the marking of something public, but here the ceremonial realm revolves chiefly around the personal. However, Newby is adept at managing that elusive skill when writing about one's own experience, that priceless knack of involving us all. And, perhaps, therein lies the brilliance of the title. Take the subtlety of the following from the opening of 'Gare Montparnasse': 'Too early, our setting off / for the station, and so long / to wait for your departure.' That phrase 'so long' is used wonderfully to dual effect when we consider it is an Americanism (Newby herself is a Los Angeles native) to refer to our more usual 'goodbye'. It could be tempting to think such an effective technique was merely chanced upon, but given the technical capability on display throughout *Ceremony*, I am going to assume that it was intended. The beauty is that it doesn't look intended.

In 'Eggplant', a daughter returns home to Los Angeles to 'no fanfare, no bank holiday'. The mother interrupts her tales of 'Grand Adventure' to lament the change in her dialect:

> ... 'O dear, how false you are! How altered!
> How can you speak that phoney English?'

This leads the daughter to concede that she too has come home and 'found things altered': 'the sad upholstery, a lock / that sticks'. One senses that given Newby undertook and completed her Ph.D. at Queen's University, Belfast, it is perhaps Belfast itself that represents the sticking lock – the tendency of a place to pull on the heart. It is a wonderful example of how travel changes us, whether we are aware of it or not, and how, usually, those closest to us are the ones that unwittingly bring us to this realisation.

There is a strikingly unerring sequence entitled 'Sixteen Glances' (perhaps a nod to the now oft-maligned coming-of-age movie *Sixteen Candles*), which is a response to Amedeo Modigliani's *Female Nude* (1916). Newby uses Modigliani's examination of the female form to examine the female condition in the twenty-first century, but also the complexity of the desire to be looked at, and yet, not objectified: 'Hearing yourself described by the person you love is mostly terrifying because it means you have been looked at – have been considered and determined by the object of your own desiring glance.' This line shook me to my senses when I read it. It is a virtuosic sequence, not least because Newby's prose poem adheres every bit to the late Ciaran Carson's assertion that prose should read as well as poetry.

Ceremony closes with a long poem entitled 'Rose Garden', which ruminates on the joy and pain of a relationship:

> Let us become a little detached, let us undertake the apprenticeship
> of a certain distance – so I tried not to talk to you.
> I tried to go elsewhere, to make an escape
> into some general image.

This is a debut pamphlet full of measured emotion, and it is refreshing to see such material staying on the right side of sentiment. The real accomplishment of *Ceremony* can be summed up in the final stanza of 'Bouquet with Flying Lovers', a poem that recounts a dream being relayed to the speaker involving a two-headed angel and a floating journey through the 'luminous blue' night sky. But which is more fantastic, the poem asks, the aforementioned, 'Or that, on waking and remembering I'm dead, / you could still smell the lilies and red roses / we upset returning through the open window?'

Grace Wilentz also explores relationships, both romantic and familial. *Holding Distance* is an assured and solidly-assembled debut pamphlet. This reviewer was particularly struck by how Wilentz is able to move so seamlessly between the tangible and the surreal. Take this fine closing line from the short prose poem 'The Iguana Dreams of Her Mom': 'I have lived through two eclipses – saw one on a beach with my mother, missed one in a dream with her too.' This surprising amalgamation of the 'real life' and the 'dream-world' is a pleasing aspect of the collection as a whole. Wilentz stays true to the title of her pamphlet, however, and does indeed 'hold her distance' with the observing eye that is the mark of good poetry.

This is beautifully demonstrated in 'The Lioness', a poem in which we are never quite sure what the setting is, the scene seemingly shifting like a dream-edit in a film, referencing a lake closed to the public, a paperback found after moving house (which could be a book of myths), culminating in the act of coupling between man and lioness:

> Her spine, curling and uncurling
>
> as she slowly departs him,
> is the most common waveform,
> the mountain system, an arc, S.

It is a strangely unsettling piece, for reasons that one doesn't fully comprehend, which, in my opinion, is the best kind of sensation when reading a poem; childhood memories of transient existence combine effortlessly with a kind of sexual realisation – the lioness is the one being entered, however she retains control, and is mythologised into the fabric of the landscape.

What ultimately marks *Holding Distance* as a debut to be savoured is the sheer deftness with which Wilentz deals with emotion. It would be all too easy to tip over into sentiment when writing about the serious illness of a loved one, but again, adhering to her pamphlet title, Wilentz uses her unerring eye to reference, in 'Cancer Diary II', 'Things that annoy you – / nakedness, / the vein of your left arm, / tapped out.' This is a marvellously moving poem about illness that never sacrifices its cold, hard observation: holding the distance, but filling it with empathy and, ultimately, love. Grace Wilentz's fine debut reminds us that despite the spaces between us we are all inevitably and inextricably linked.

Louise G Cole's *Soft Touch* was a Laureate's Choice, chosen by the former Poet Laureate Carol Ann Duffy, so I was keen to get between its covers, and it did not disappoint. Like McKendry's *Curfuffle*, Cole writes with a swagger that belies the title: it is apparent from the outset that the author is no 'soft touch'. In the opening poem, 'Fur Coat and No Knickers', the speaker visits her ninety-two-year-old mother who is beset with what one assumes is dementia, or a related condition:

> I get up to leave and the frail old cripple
> who used to be my mother

>   spills her tea and demands
>   to know when cousin Betty intends returning
>   the fur coat, says quietly: "I always knew
>   what a little whore you were."

Cole competently and admirably weaves humour throughout the poem, without ever relinquishing the gravity of the situation, which means that those final quoted lines pack all the more powerful a punch.

In 'Growing Boobs', we are challenged to consider whether a 'little grey pervy bloke' should be let off the hook due to his old age, despite his leering behaviour which the poet recalls from her teenage job at the deli counter in Woolworths; he asks for 'exactly seven and a half ounces / of mature farmhouse cheddar // *that's what they'd weigh*, he'd say / staring at my teenage chest as I / positioned the cheese-wire, *each*'. The poet is told not to mind, that the man in question was 'probably / a war hero'. Where do we draw the line in relation to unacceptably invasive behaviour? It is a necessary discussion. Again, Cole dares us to snigger, but keeps us firmly in her gaze.

What pleased me most about *Soft Touch* was the rhythm and flow of the language. Take the opening lines from 'Watermarked': 'The teeming river's upright heron casts / my father: alert, slim and spike-beaked'. The five-beat-per-line rhythm imitates the river itself, wonderfully fusing the image of the heron with the image of the speaker's father in a manner that is as heartbreaking as it is striking. Cole gets to the meat and mire of the human condition in *Soft Touch*, which is what one can only hope to aspire to in any creative endeavour.

Helen Meany

FROM DAY TO DAY

Catherine Phil MacCarthy, *Daughters of the House* (Dedalus Press, 2019), €12.50.
Enda Wyley, *The Painter on his Bike* (Dedalus Press, 2019), €12.50.
Macdara Woods, *Music From the Big Tent* (Dedalus Press, 2016), €12.50.

In these strange days in March, with thoughts of quarantine, retreat, and self-isolation never far away, the chance to travel freely in the mind – into the past, or to Paris, Umbria, or the Bosphorus – comes as a gift, in three collections from Dedalus Press. Two were published last year, by Enda Wyley and Catherine Phil MacCarthy, and the third is the final collection by the late poet, editor, and translator, Macdara Woods.

A residency at the Centre Culturel Irlandais in Paris gave Catherine Phil MacCarthy the time and space to delve into the work of female artists who had lived in the city a century earlier. A core group of poems in this award-winning writer's fifth collection connects the impulse towards women's artistic and personal freedom in the late-nineteenth and early-twentieth century with the Irish nationalist movement and the Celtic Revival. The painter Sarah Purser is a central figure here, with poems responding to her portraits of Maud Gonne and Michael Davitt. Not strictly speaking ekphrastic, these poems take Purser's paintings as a starting point for glowing vignettes. These in turn give rise to biographical poems about Gonne, Davitt, and his wife Mary Yore, creating a rich series of correspondences and echoes, including quotations from letters from Davitt to Purser.

The young Miss Gonne enters the frame: 'Though high and solitary, she is not yet stern', but, at the age of 23, 'a cameo of pensiveness.' And on her mind, memories of:

> Emergency men
> with battering ram, smashing down doors.
> Cries of a newborn, locked in her throat.
> – 'SARAH PURSER'S *LADY WITH A MONKEY, A PORTRAIT*'

The transition from the playful Yeatsian reference to an image of violence is typical of the deftness and poise of this historical sequence, which stands out from the more observational poems in this collection, evoking the natural world and family relationships.

Traces of architect Eileen Gray are summoned in '21, rue Bonaparte', as well as, in 'A Marketable Craft', the Russian painter Marie Bashkirtseff, who died of TB aged 25, leaving a posthumously-published diary. Always, a feminist consciousness is to the fore, with the imperative to be self-reliant, as in 'Paris Diary':

> ... words
>
> written long ago echoed a sacred vow:
> I need but two dark blouses a year,
> a change of linen that I could wash myself,
>
> the simplest food fresh from the garden
> and the means to work; this is all.

The rough edges of the artist's life poke through 'Painter's Model', written in memory of Wally Neuzil, the teenage model in many of Egon Schiele's drawings and paintings, including *Death and the Maiden* (1915): 'She became / the woman with red lips, tawny hair, // raised knees, black stockings'; while 'She kept house, / framed prints, saw clients, sold new work, / paid the rent, slept alone'.

In three linked poems, 'Land League Cottage', we hear the voice of Mary Yore, homesick for her Californian girlhood, left behind with their children as Davitt sets off for London, to his other life as a public man. Written in elegant couplets, this affecting triptych and the poem that follows, 'Wedding Song', evoke marital love and tenderness without ever being mawkish.

Enda Wyley also succeeds in achieving that fine balance, as amply demonstrated in her sixth collection, *The Painter on his Bike*. With poems for her daughter ('Tree House'), in memory of her parents ('Home'), and elegies for recently deceased friends, such as 'To the Core', it places love and friendship at its heart. And, like MacCarthy's *Daughters of the House*, the collection brims with references and responses to work by painters and sculptors, among Wyley's circle of friends and acquaintances. These include the title poem, written for the artist James Hanley, cycling home with his portrait of his dead father balanced on his lap, 'bumping over / potholes and tramlines, // the picture beating / against his knee'.

Wyley's touch is so light – the two-line stanzas she favours scattering images, then gathering them in – that the craft is masked, revealing itself on re-reading. Later, she moves from the deceptively casual, paired short lines to a tauter form, as in the highly compressed 'Text', capturing the experience of reading and sending a text message:

> A beep and I reply,
> imagining your hands,

> somewhere else,
> reaching up to catch
> my words back to you.
> A house destroyed,
> a river path overgrown,
> conservatory glass
> all shattered, a walled
> garden locked, the past
> drowning, but this text
> grasps at the future,
> is what was and cannot
> be forgotten.

Grasping at the future with courage becomes a theme, with a number of poems recalling her husband Peter Sirr's hospitalisation, and the relief of his recovery, as she addresses him in the short sequence 'Walks': 'On the lane to Rath I see you now / illness a coat tossed over the hedgerow – / and you striding into evening's soft relief.'

In the marvellous 'Ledger', their love story is given an epic, romantic treatment. With its dedication to Peter Sirr, it shows one poet answering another, with poetry translating into action in the most direct and immediate way, propelling Wyley out onto the street to find him. She describes the moment when she first came across his collection, *The Ledger of Fruitful Exchange*, which:

> ... thrilled, made me stand up in the bookshop,
>
> then make for the door, our future racing out onto
> Dawson Street and into the city's expanse,
> Larkin raising his hands to me, the gulls cawing
>
> encouragement as I sought you out, your face staring
> from a high window over Parnell Square, the life
> you'd described becoming ours, the door unlatched.

Memories of the couple's past are tinged with an awareness of the fragility of things in a sequence of terse 'Short Love Poems'. Likewise, in a moving reading of the myth of Orpheus in the Underworld, voiced from Eurydice's point of view, she realises instantly that the lovers will be separated forever: 'One look from you and I know this' ('Eurydice Speaks').

Memories of childhood, of empty rooms and houses thread through the later poems, with an accumulating awareness of absences and loss, of ghosts:

> A hand not there, a person unseen, the window
> sprung open for one reason – that I should see
> what I hadn't before, get up and go outside.
> – 'GHOST MESSAGE'

This spirit of curiosity, of open receptivity, pervades the collection, which is also, *inter alia*, a celebration of Dublin.

A readily recognisable figure on the streets of Dublin, Macdara Woods (1942-2018) was a writer whose sensibility and outlook were always international, while being rooted in Ireland. His was an influential voice in Irish poetry from the 1970s onwards, as co-founder and editor of *Cyphers* magazine and as mentor to younger poets, as well as through workshops, readings, and multiple collections, most of which were published by Dedalus Press, including his *Collected Poems* in 2012.

Music From the Big Tent reflects Woods's breadth of interests, wide travels, and the enduring importance of music in his work, with a number of the poems in ballad form, their titles referring to traditional songs and jazz. A pivotal sequence reflects on his experience of serious illness and of slow, painful recovery: the ageing body, and the inevitability of death.

The most finely-crafted poems are less directly autobiographical but reflect on time and distance: responding to a painting in the enigmatic 'Members Of The Sheridan Family In The National Gallery'; or to an image recovered from distant memory in 'My Degas Words' and 'In Tomis He Remembers', both highly distilled, in short lines weighted with 'the floating / rocketry and stamina / of centuries'. They convey a sense of the poet reaching for a word or image just outside of reach, 'Which I so want to see / up close / because it looks so easy // From afar / as all art does – except / for love' ('My Degas Words'). And again, there's the search for the precise moment that can ignite a poem: 'Such memories that are I feel / Of things that never were // But being true / to them / without traduction ... is how the poetry works / And how the tangent comes to touch / Some point of contact that fires the spark' ('Nerium: Hiroshima Day 2015').

In hospital in Dublin, re-learning how to walk, he envisions a return to Perugia, Umbria, his family's home from home. Remembering his own father's last days in the scrupulously spare, caesura-studded stanzas of 'Sons Are Older At The Speed Of Light', he knows that they are both 'Poor transients':

> And one day indeed the words ran out
> And we   with nothing   left to say
> Consulted over menus
> Read bits of news   repeated saws

> To get us through the silence – you
> Didn't know
>   And I had yet to learn
> That few words   A simple few
> Could be enough   could tell it all

And finally, these eloquently halting lines come to a close:

>   We last from day to day
> No more than that   That's it   Enough
> For now
> The diagnosis works   Of course it does:
> Whoever died a winter yet?

Derek Mahon

EVERYTHING IS GOING TO BE ALL RIGHT

How should I not be glad to contemplate
the clouds clearing beyond the dormer window
and a high tide reflected on the ceiling?
There will be dying, there will be dying,
but there is no need to go into that.
The lines flow from the hand unbidden
and the hidden source is the watchful heart;
the sun rises in spite of everything
and the far cities are beautiful and bright.
I lie here in a riot of sunlight
watching the day break and the clouds flying.
Everything is going to be all right.

'Everything Is Going to Be All Right' by Derek Mahon from *New Selected Poems* (2016), reproduced by kind permission of the author and The Gallery Press.

Notes on Contributors

Tá dhá chnuasach ag **Michael Begnal**, *Future Blues* (Salmon Poetry, 2012) agus *Ancestor Worship* (Salmon Poetry, 2007). He was co-founder of the original *Burning Bush* journal.

Tara Bergin has published two poetry collections with Carcanet Press, *This is Yarrow* (2013), winner of the Seamus Heaney Prize and Shine/Strong Award, and *The Tragic Death of Eleanor Marx* (2017), shortlisted for the TS Eliot and Forward Prizes. 'Home-schooling', in this issue, was written following the closure of schools due to coronavirus, and was inspired by the *Key Stage Two English Grammar, Punctuation and Spelling* workbook.

Sharon Black is from Glasgow and lives in France. She won The Guernsey International Poetry Competition 2019, and *The London Magazine* Poetry Prize, 2018 and 2019. Her two collections are *To Know Bedrock* (Pindrop Press, 2011) and *The Art of Egg* (Two Ravens Press, 2015; Pindrop Press, 2019). Her third collection is forthcoming from TLM Editions.

Liam Carson is the director of the IMRAM Irish Language Literature Festival, and the author of the memoir *call mother a lonely field*. He has just finished writing a collection of haiku.

Máirtín Coilféir is from Co Meath, currently living in Canada. He has published work in *The Stinging Fly*, *Gorse*, and the bilingual poetry anthology *Calling Cards* (The Gallery Press/Poetry Ireland, 2019). His first monograph, *Titley* (Leabhair Comhar, 2019), is available now.

Henri Cole was born in Fukuoka, Japan. His most recent book is *Orphic Paris*, a memoir. His tenth collection of poetry, *Blizzard*, is forthcoming from Farrar, Straus and Giroux.

Emily S Cooper has been published in *The Stinging Fly*, *Banshee*, *The Irish Times*, *Hotel*, and elsewhere. She was awarded residencies by the Arts Council of Northern Ireland, Greywood Arts, and the Irish Writers' Centre. In 2019, she took part in Poetry Ireland's Introductions series, and was a recipient of the Next Generation Award from the Arts Council of Ireland. Her first poetry pamphlet will be published by Makina Books in 2020. She lives in Donegal, and is currently writing a monograph on solitude.

Simon Costello's poetry has appeared in *The Honest Ulsterman*, *The Irish Times*, *The North*, *Rattle*, *The Stinging Fly*, and *The Tangerine*. He was shortlisted for the 2018 Red Line Book Festival Poetry Competition, and in 2019 he was one of the Hennessy / *Irish Times* New Irish Writing winners. He features in *The Best New British and Irish Poets 2019-2020* (Eyewear Publishing).

Greg Delanty's most recent book is *The Greek Anthology, Book XVII* (Carcanet Press). He is Poet in Residence at Saint Michael's College, Vermont. He has two books forthcoming this year, a book of his own work, *No More Time* (LSU Press), and a selected Seán Ó Ríordáin titled *Apathy Is Out* (Bloodaxe Books).

Susannah Dickey's most recent pamphlet is *bloodthirsty for marriage* (Bad Betty Press, 2020). Her second pamphlet, *genuine human values* (The Lifeboat, 2018), won the 2019 Vincent Buckley Poetry Prize. Her debut novel, *Tennis Lessons*, will be published by Doubleday in July.

Katherine Duffy's most recent poetry publication is *Talking the Owl Away* (Templar Poetry, 2018), which won Templar's Iota Shot Pamphlet Award in 2018. Two previous collections were published by Dedalus Press. She is also an award-winning fiction writer and translator.

Susan Millar DuMars has published five collections with Salmon Poetry. The most recent, *Naked: New and Selected Poems*, came out in 2019. The book celebrates Susan's twenty-five years as a published poet. Born in Philadelphia, Susan lives in Galway, where she teaches creative writing and has coordinated and hosted the Over the Edge readings series since 2003.

Martina Evans is the author of eleven books of poetry and prose. Her latest collection, *Now We Can Talk Openly About Men*, was published by Carcanet Press in 2018, and was shortlisted for *The Irish Times* Poetry Now Award, The Roehampton Poetry Prize, and The Pigott Poetry Prize.

Rebecca Morgan Frank is the author of four collections of poems, including *Oh You Robot Saints*, forthcoming from Carnegie Mellon University Press in 2021, and *Little Murders Everywhere* (Salmon Poetry, 2012), a finalist for the Kate Tufts Discovery Award. Her poems have appeared in *The New Yorker*, *American Poetry Review*, and elsewhere.

Tom French's books are published by The Gallery Press.

Alan Gillis was born in Belfast, and now lives and teaches in Edinburgh. His new poetry collection, *The Readiness*, is published this year by Picador Poetry. He is the author of four previous poetry collections with The Gallery Press.

Nicholas Grene is Emeritus Professor of English Literature at Trinity College, Dublin, and a Member of the Royal Irish Academy. His books include *The Politics of Irish Drama* (Cambridge University Press, 1999), *Yeats's Poetic Codes* (Oxford University Press, 2008), *The Oxford Handbook of Modern Irish Theatre* (Oxford University Press, 2016) co-edited with Chris Morash, and *The Theatre of Tom Murphy: Playwright Adventurer* (Bloomsbury, 2017). He is currently writing a book on farming in modern Irish literature, to be published by Oxford University Press in 2021.

India Harris was born in Devon and now lives in Belfast. She studied at Girton College, Cambridge, and the Seamus Heaney Centre for Poetry at Queen's University, Belfast. She is currently pursuing a Ph.D. in poetry criticism.

Eleanor Hooker's third poetry collection, *Mending the Light*, is forthcoming. She is founder and curator of the Rowan Tree Readings. She is helm, and edits rescue footage, for Lough Derg RNLI lifeboat. Eleanor is a Fellow of the Linnean Society of London.

Benjamin Keatinge is a Visiting Research Fellow at the School of English, Trinity College, Dublin. He has edited *Making Integral: Critical Essays on Richard Murphy* (Cork University Press, 2019), and his poetry has appeared in *Agenda, Orbis, Eborakon, The Galway Review, Cassandra Voices, Flare*, and in *Writing Home: The 'New Irish' Poets* (Dedalus Press, 2019).

John Kelly's first collection of poetry, *Notions*, was published by Dedalus Press in 2018. His work has appeared in *The Irish Times, Poetry Ireland Review, Winter Papers, The Stinging Fly, Banshee, The Well Review, The Moth, Oxford Magazine*, and several anthologies. A novel, *From Out of the City*, was shortlisted for Novel of the Year at the Irish Book Awards 2014. A radio play, *The Pipes*, was broadcast on RTÉ.

Erik Kennedy is the author of *There's No Place Like the Internet in Springtime* (Victoria University Press, 2018). His poetry and criticism have recently been published in places like *B O D Y, The Dark Horse, The Manchester Review, The Moth, POETRY,* and the *TLS*. He lives in Christchurch, New Zealand.

Zaffar Kunial's *Us* (Faber and Faber, 2018) was shortlisted for the Costa Poetry Award and the TS Eliot Prize. He was writer in residence at the Brontë Parsonage Museum, and explored the life of Patrick Brontë. He is currently the Douglas Caster Fellow in Poetry at Leeds University. A pamphlet, *Six*, was published by Faber and Faber in 2019.

Michael Longley has received many awards, among them the TS Eliot Prize and The Queen's Gold Medal for Poetry. In 2015 he was made a Freeman of the City of Belfast, where he and his wife, the critic Edna Longley, live and work. His twelfth collection, *The Candlelight Master*, is forthcoming from Jonathan Cape in August.

Mícheál McCann is from Derry. His poems appear in *Poetry Ireland Review*, *Banshee Lit*, and the Poetry Jukebox. He was a grateful recipient of an Arts Council of Northern Ireland ACES Award in 2019, and his first pamphlet of poems is forthcoming this year from Green Bottle Press.

Afric McGlinchey is the author of *The lucky star of hidden things* (Salmon Poetry and, in Italian, L'Arcolaio), *Ghost of the Fisher Cat* (Salmon Poetry, and forthcoming in Italian), and *Invisible Insane* (SurVision Books). Her honours include a Hennessy/*Irish Times* Award, an Arts Council bursary, and Pushcart Prize and Best of the Net nominations.

Ruth McIlroy's pamphlet *Guppy Primer* was the Poetry Book Society's Pamphlet Choice for Winter 2017. She has been published in magazines including *The Poetry Review* and *The Manchester Review*, and read at the launch of *The Poetry Review* in April 2018. She lives in Yorkshire.

Elizabeth McIntosh received a Master's in Irish Writing from Trinity College, Dublin in 2018. She currently lives in California and serves as a poetry editor for *Crack the Spine*. Her poems have appeared in *Smithereens*, the *HCE Review*, and *The Wildean*.

Paul Maddern has four publications with Templar Poetry, the latest being *The Tipping Line* (2018). He received two Bermuda Government Literary Awards, for *The Beachcomber's Report* (2010), and *Pilgrimage* (2017). Having taught at Leeds University and Queen's University, Belfast, he now owns and operates The River Mill writers' retreat in Co Down.

Derek Mahon's most recent collection, *Against the Clock*, received the *Irish Times* Poetry Now Award last year, the third time he'd received this award. The Gallery Press looks forward to publishing a new collection, *Washing Up*, in October.

Michael Martin's first poetry collection, *Extended Remark: Poems From A Moravian Parking Lot*, was published by Portals Press (New Orleans, 2015). His poems have appeared widely, including in *American Journal of Poetry*, *RHINO*, *Nine Mile Magazine*, *New Orleans Review*, *Carolina Quarterly*, and *Berkeley Poetry Review*. For a decade, he lived in the Netherlands, where he was a feature writer and Contributing Editor with *Amsterdam Weekly*. He lives now in North Carolina with his wife and sons.

Helen Meany is a culture writer and arts consultant, and theatre critic for Ireland for *The Guardian*. She was Literature Advisor to the Arts Council, 2011-18, and Curator of the Arts Council's Critical Voices programme, 2005-6. She was editor of *Irish Theatre Magazine* (2005-11), and an arts journalist and commissioning editor with *The Irish Times* (1991-2002).

Julie Morrissy is an Irish poet, academic, critic, and activist. Her first collection *Where, the Mile End* (2019) is published by Book*hug (Canada) and tall-lighthouse (UK). She is the first Newman Fellow in Creativity at University College Dublin.

Eiléan Ní Chuilleanáin is an Emeritus Fellow of Trinity College, Dublin. She has published nine collections of poetry, and was Ireland Chair of Poetry (2016-2019). Her latest collection, *The Mother House* (The Gallery Press, 2019), received the *Irish Times*/Poetry Now Award, 2020.

Doireann Ní Ghríofa's most recent book of poems is *Lies* (Dedalus Press), an *Irish Times* Book of the Year and an *Irish Independent* Book of 2018. Awards for her writing include a Lannan Literary Fellowship, a Seamus Heaney Fellowship, and the Rooney Prize for Irish Literature.

Stiofán Ó Cadhla was born in Ring, Co Waterford and raised both there and in Cork city. He is a Senior Lecturer in Roinn an Bhéaloidis / The Department of Folklore and Ethnology in UCC. Along with many publications in his field he has published three collections of poetry in Irish, *An Creideamhach Déanach* (Coiscéim, 2009), *Tarraing na Cuirtíní, a Dhochtúir* (Coiscéim, 2012), and *Rialacha Nua an Scuaine* (Coiscéim, 2017). He was awarded the Gradam Filíochta Mhichíl Uí hAirtnéide/Michael Hartnett Award in 2012.

Nessa O'Mahony has published five volumes of poetry, the most recent being *The Hollow Woman on the Island* (Salmon Poetry, 2019). She is co-editor with Siobhán Campbell of *Eavan Boland: Inside History* (Arlen House, 2016) a volume of essays and poetry responding to the work of Eavan Boland.

Cathal Ó Searcaigh was born and grew up on a hill farm in Mín an Leá, Gort an Choirce, an Irish-speaking glen and Gaeltacht community in the northwest of Co Donegal. He is the author of 17 volumes of poetry, three plays, and four works of prose in Irish, as well as four books in English. He is a leading figure in the remarkable renaissance of Irish-language writing in our time. A member of Aosdána, he continues to live on the home ground of his parents.

Keith Payne was the Ireland Chair of Poetry Bursary Award winner for 2015-2016. His collection *Broken Hill* (Lapwing Publications, 2015), was followed by *Six Galician Poets* (Arc Publications, 2016), and, from the Galego of Martín Veiga, *Diary of Crosses Green* (Francis Boutle Publishers, 2018). He is director of the 'La Malinche' Readings Ireland/Galicia, and of the PoemaRia Poetry festival in Vigo.

Michael Prior's poems have appeared in *The New Republic*, POETRY, *PN Review*, *Ambit*, *The Manchester Review*, and the Academy of American Poets' Poem-a-Day series. A past winner of Magma Poetry's Editors' Prize, his second book of poems, *Burning Province*, is forthcoming from McClelland & Stewart/Penguin Random House.

Liz Quirke is a poet and scholar from Kerry. She teaches on the MA in Writing at NUI Galway. Salmon Poetry published her debut collection *The Road, Slowly* in 2018, and will publish her second collection, *How We Arrive In Winter*, in late 2020.

Matthew Rice was born in Belfast. His poems have appeared in *Asheville Poetry Review*, *Poetry Ireland Review*, *The Tangerine*, and in the anthology *The Best New British and Irish Poets 2017*. He was awarded runner-up in the Seamus Heaney Award for New Writing 2017, and selected for the Poetry Ireland Introductions Series the same year. He received a SIAP award from the Arts Council of Northern Ireland for 2017/18.

Gabriel Rosenstock is a poet, tankaist, and haikuist, whose latest titles are *Walk with Gandhi: Bóthar na Saoirse* (Gandhi 150 Ireland), *Glengower: Poems for No One in Irish and English* (The Onslaught Press, 2018), *An Eala Órga* (An Gúm, 2019), retellings of tales from India, and a bilingual edition in Sanskrit and Irish of an Advaitic scripture, *Aṣṭāvakra Gītā*.

Lorna Shaughnessy has published three poetry collections with Salmon Poetry, *Torching the Brown River*, *Witness Trees*, and *Anchored*, and a chapbook, *Song of the Forgotten Shulamite*, with Lapwing Publications. *Lark Water*, her fourth collection, will be launched in 2020. She lectures in Hispanic Studies in NUI Galway and translates Spanish and Latin American poetry.

Kathryn Simmonds lives with her family in Norwich. Her poetry collections are *Sunday at the Skin Launderette* (2008) and *The Visitations* (2013), both published by Seren Books. She is finishing a third collection.

Gerard Smyth's most recent collections are *The Sundays of Eternity* and *A Song of Elsewhere*, both from Dedalus Press. *The Fullness of Time: New and Selected Poems* was published by Dedalus Press in 2010. He is a member of Aosdána and Poetry Editor of *The Irish Times*.

David Toms lives and works in Oslo, Norway. His most recent collection of poetry is *Northly*, from Turas Press.

Molly Twomey holds an MA in Creative Writing from UCC, and was published by *Banshee*, *The Irish Times*, *Crannóg*, and on educate.ie, among other outlets. She won the New Voices section in The Voices of War International Poetry Competition (UCD), and in 2019 she won the Padraic Colum Poetry Prize and came second in the Waterford Poetry Prize.

As Gaoth Dobhair i dTír Chonaill don fhile agus gearrscéalaí **Máire Dinny Wren**. D'fhoilsigh Coiscéim a céad bailiúchán filíochta, *Ó Bhile go Bile*, in 2011. In 2016, d'fhoilsigh Éabhlóid, a céad cnuasacht gearrscéalta, *Go mbeinnse choíche saor*, agus a dara cnuasach filíochta, *Tine Ghealáin*, in 2019. Tá saothair léi foilsithe in irisí ar nós *Duillí Éireann*, *Comhar*, *an tUltach*, *Feasta*, *Poblachd nam Bàrd*, *The Bramley Flash Fiction Anthology*, *Strokestown Poetry Anthology 3*, agus tá ceithre scéal dá cuid sa chnuasacht *Go dtí an lá bán* a d'fhoilsigh
Éabhlóid in 2012.

Editors, *Poetry Ireland Review*

John Jordan 1–8	Spring 1981–Autumn 1983
Thomas McCarthy 9–12	Winter 1983–Winter 1984
Conleth Ellis and Rita E Kelly 13	Spring 1985
Terence Brown 14–17	Autumn 1985–Autumn 1986
Ciaran Cosgrove 18–19	Spring 1987
Dennis O'Driscoll 20–21	Autumn 1987–Spring 1988
John Ennis and Rory Brennan 22–23	Summer 1988
John Ennis 24–25	Winter 1988–Spring 1989
Michael O'Siadhail 26–29	Summer 1989–Summer 1990
Máire Mhac an tSaoi 30–33	Autumn 1990–Winter 1991
Peter Denman 34–37	Spring 1992–Winter 1992
Pat Boran 38	Summer 1993
Seán Ó Cearnaigh 39	Autumn 1993
Pat Boran 40–42	Winter 1993–Summer 1994
Chris Agee 43–44	Autumn–Winter 1994
Moya Cannon 45–48	Spring 1995–Winter 1995
Liam Ó Muirthile 49	Spring 1996
Michael Longley 50	Summer 1996
Liam Ó Muirthile 51–52	Autumn 1996–Spring 1997
Frank Ormsby 53–56	Summer 1997–Spring 1998
Catherine Phil MacCarthy 57–60	Summer 1998–Spring 1999
Mark Roper 61–64	Summer 1999–Spring 2000
Biddy Jenkinson 65–68	Summer 2000–Spring 2001
Maurice Harmon 69–72	Summer 2001–Spring 2002
Michael Smith 73–75	Summer 2002–Winter 2002
Eva Bourke 76	Spring/Summer 2003
Peter Sirr 77–91	Autumn 2003–October 2007
Eiléan Ní Chuilleanáin 92–95	December 2007–October 2008
Caitríona O'Reilly 96–99	December 2008–October 2009
Paul Muldoon 100	March 2010
Caitríona O'Reilly 101–104	July 2010–September 2011
John F Deane 105–112	December 2011–April 2014
Vona Groarke 113–120	September 2014–December 2016
Eavan Boland 121-129	April 2017–December 2019